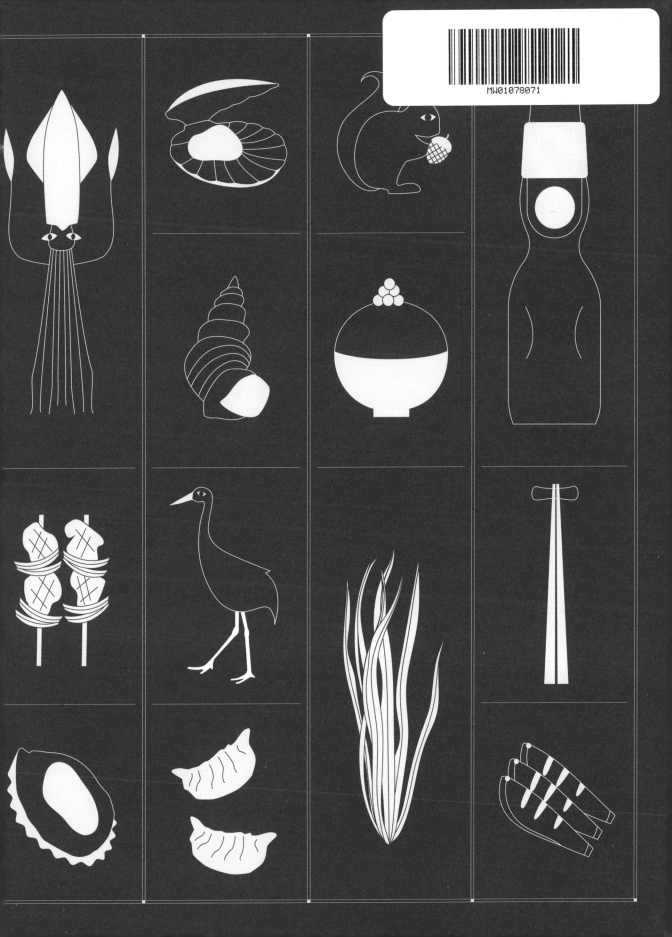

**FOR TIG AND FELIX
MAY YOU FALL IN LOVE SOMEDAY**

北海道
HOKKAIDO

RECIPES FROM THE SEAS, FIELDS AND FARMLANDS OF NORTHERN JAPAN

TIM ANDERSON

Hardie Grant

BOOKS

MAP OF HOKKAIDO

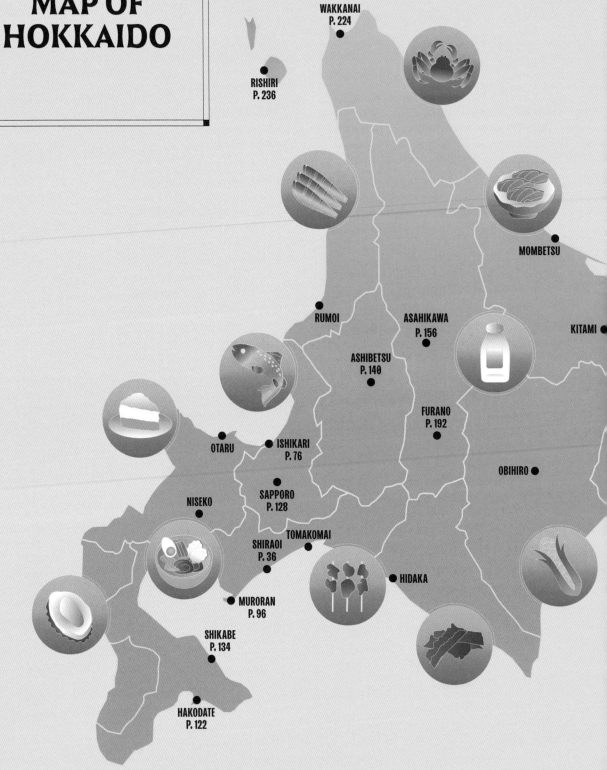

WAKKANAI
P. 224

RISHIRI
P. 236

MOMBETSU

RUMOI

ASAHIKAWA
P. 156

KITAMI

ASHIBETSU
P. 140

FURANO
P. 192

OTARU

ISHIKARI
P. 76

OBIHIRO

NISEKO

SAPPORO
P. 128

TOMAKOMAI

SHIRAOI
P. 36

HIDAKA

MURORAN
P. 96

SHIKABE
P. 134

HAKODATE
P. 122

CONTENTS

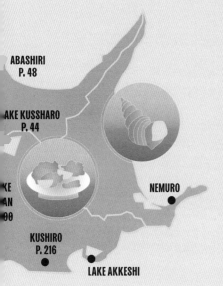

ABASHIRI
P. 48

AKE KUSSHARO
P. 44

KE
AN
00

NEMURO

KUSHIRO
P. 216

LAKE AKKESHI

IRANKA

WELCOME TO

RAPTE! *

*'Hello!' in Ainu

HOKKAIDO

北海道へようこそ

DON'T CALL IT A FRONTIER

RECENTRING JAPANESE CUISINE

It's tempting to describe Hokkaido – Japan's northernmost island – as a 'frontier'. This is the language used by Hokkaido's own tourism organisation, a slogan proudly displayed above photos of the island's undeniably beautiful scenery: 'Japan's Northern Frontier'. Hokkaido was officially claimed by the imperial Japanese government in 1869, following the Meiji Restoration the previous year. The annexation invites comparisons between Hokkaido and the American West, and the American idea of 'manifest destiny'. It was considered a logical and obvious step, taken to consolidate power, protect the country against Russia, and complete the Japanese mainland we all recognise today. I must say that historical maps of Japan without Hokkaido look funny to me – like the country is missing its head.

I, too, have often thought of Hokkaido as a frontier. But I am mindful of historian Brett L. Walker's explanation of why this is problematic. In *The Conquest of Ainu Lands,* he writes:

> '... as a conceptual tool, the notion of the frontier peripheralizes Ezo [Hokkaido's pre-Meiji name] ... trade, cultural interaction, economic growth, and state expansion in Ezo are often cast as part of the pageantry of Japanese national progress, rather than as the subjugation of the Ainu homeland.' [1]

Positioning Hokkaido as a frontier is to portray the island as historically empty, land that was simply 'discovered' by the imperial government. The reality is that Hokkaido was already home to the Ainu and other indigenous groups for centuries. Their land was taken, and they were forced to assimilate into Japanese society under a series of harsh laws that banned Ainu cultural practices.

When I was a student, I more or less bought into the mainstream narrative of the imperial 'development' (*kaitaku*) of Hokkaido. On a research trip in 2005, this was indelibly illustrated to me at the Sapporo Beer Museum, of all places: essentially a glorified brewery tour, which merrily tells the story of modern Hokkaido in diorama form. Vignettes of farming, brewing and city-building are positioned along a sparkling river of beer representing the force of history – the transformation of dry grains and bitter flowers into delicious lager as metaphor for the transformation of untamed land into civilisation.

It's all too easy to get swept up along this river of beer, in a feeling of enterprise and endeavour that calls to mind Hokkaido's unofficial motto:

'Boys, be ambitious!' 「少年よ、大志を抱け!」

These words were famously spoken by William S. Clark, an American professor enlisted by the Japanese government to advise on Western farming methods and to help establish the Sapporo Agricultural College (now Hokkaido University) in the 1870s. Dr Clark became an enduring symbol of Hokkaido's pioneer spirit, and throughout the prefecture you'll find many buildings that bear his name, many busts and statues that bear his likeness.

The most famous one is at Hitsujigaoka in Sapporo, with his famous quote etched at its base. Clark appears larger than life, cast in bronze, arm outstretched, gesturing towards the future. His overcoat flaps in the breeze, like a superhero's cape. A steady stream of buses stop at Hitsujigaoka to deposit tourists and school groups who come to have their photo taken in front of Clark's iconic image. They stand before him and proudly emulate his pose, uplifted by his stirring words. '*Boys, be ambitious.*'

The culinary landscape of Hokkaido as we know it today is a product of so many ambitious boys, and their efforts to colonise, monetise and fortify the island within the broader military-industrial expansion of Japan. Many of the things Hokkaido is now best known for – milk, lamb, sweetcorn and beer, to name a few – were introduced as part of the European-style agriculture that Clark and his contemporaries initiated, to make the most of a climate and terrain which is mostly unsuitable for rice growing.

Foods such as these were an important part of what interested me in Hokkaido in the first place. They reminded me of home – of Wisconsin, 'America's Dairyland'. And the whole mythos of being ambitious, cultivating the land in order to make money and eat cheese. Well, it's the American dream! It resonated all too well with me. Wisconsin even has its own short-and-sweet motto to rival Dr Clark's: '*Forward!*'

But you don't have to be from Wisconsin to find plenty to love about Hokkaido and its food. The sweetest melons, the freshest crab, an ever-expanding universe of buttery pastries ... and the list goes on. In a country filled with great food, Hokkaido is, without a doubt, my favourite place to eat.

Food can be used for escapism – which I fully endorse – and Hokkaido offers countless opportunities for this. I am an anxious person, and an emotional eater. These two things are not always immediately connected, but they often are. Food has the power to take me out of my own brain for a moment, commanding my attention to focus on what I'm eating. In Hokkaido, this could be a luxurious caramel walnut cake, or the scalding hot lard on top of a bowl of ramen, or the intense flavour of salted salmon kidneys. I eat these things, and I stop worrying for a moment. And I truly love them for that.

But while escapism is great, why stop there? We can enjoy the mood-altering, sensory magic of food while also learning the histories behind it. Sometimes, those histories can be heartbreaking – such as the displacement and disenfranchisement of the Ainu. But that knowledge also presents more opportunities: to learn, to course-correct, to deepen and complicate our understanding.

Efforts are sometimes made to assert the importance of Hokkaido's culinary output by noting its influence on mainstream Japanese cuisine. A frequently cited example is how the export of kombu from Hokkaido to Kyoto formed one of the most fundamental pillars of Japanese gastronomy. But Hokkaido doesn't need to justify itself in this way. The food of Hokkaido is important not because of how it has been received elsewhere, but because of how it has sustained the people of Hokkaido themselves. It is our privilege to partake in it, and to learn from it.

ABOUT THIS BOOK

You could pick any one sub-category of Hokkaido food – ramen, soup curry, Ainu cooking, cheese, etc. – and write a whole book just on that, and still not cover everything. This book is not to be taken as encyclopaedic or definitive.

From a local's perspective, there may be a dearth of Hokkaido-style home cooking and too much emphasis on *omiyage* and restaurant dishes. From a visitor's perspective, there are likely to be other glaring omissions – such as food from popular destinations like Otaru or Niseko. There is also the whole world of Ainu food, an enormous topic in and of itself, which is barely introduced here (pages 17–43). I have compiled a list of resources on page 244, so please do have a look to learn more.

The recipes mostly fall into two categories. The first are regional dishes with many variations. For these, I have done my best to come up with a recipe that synthesises those variations in order to create a representative version of the dish. The other category may be described as homages, or copycats, based on specific dishes that are unique to particular shops. The versions presented here are my best (educated) guesses to try and recreate the dishes as accurately as I can.

Familiarity with Japanese ingredients and basic techniques is assumed. If there are terms that are new to you, look them up on the internet! For all its faults, the internet remains pretty good at answering questions.

This book contains words from the Ainu language, which have been romanised according to a standard set by the National Ainu Museum. However, please note that this standard does not match Japanese romanisation in terms of pronunciation, and Ainu is a geographically diverse language with many variants. It is not possible to provide even a basic introduction to the Ainu language here, but if you would like to learn more about it, there is a very useful guide by Kane Kumagai, called 'Ainu for Beginners', which can be accessed at Unilang.org.[2]

ACKNOWLEDGEMENTS

This book has relied upon the hard work and generosity of so many people, whom I want to acknowledge up front.

First and foremost I must thank Miho Oguri, my contact at the JNTO. Miho was so dedicated to this book and the research that went into it that it feels appropriate to call her a partner. Miho, I am so grateful for all your help, and I hope I have done you proud.

Miho also connected me to my visa sponsors: Michael Stock of Japan-San, and Hideo Shōji and Mari Momiki of Mitate. Thank you so much for hosting me; your hospitality was a moving re-introduction to real *omotenashi* and I will always remember our brief time together.

My research would have been fundamentally flawed if it did not include the perspectives of Ainu people and people who know Ainu food intimately, and for this I am enormously thankful to Ryōko Tahara, Akira Toko, Yoshifuru Gōukon, Hiromi Isori, Keiko Saitō and Hiroaki Kon. Your insights have given me a deeper and more nuanced understanding of Ainu cuisine. I appreciate your honesty and your personal, good-humoured responses to my questions. My sincere thanks also go to Dr Mio Yachita and Tomoko Ōkawa for their guidance at Upopoy, and to Chef Yōsuke Mori and Upopoy's Ainu cookery instructors (who I only knew by their nicknames, Arawanatuy Sensei and Riruyika Sensei) for teaching me so much about Ainu dishes, ingredients and techniques.

I also relied on the guidance of local officials throughout Hokkaido. In Shikabe, my thanks go to Hajime Okada and Tasuku Kanazawa for showing me around their beautiful town, as well as Īda-san, the kombu farmer, and Toshiko 'Toshi-chan' Yoshida for her chanchan-yaki lesson. In Kushiro and Akan, I must thank Yuki Ōno for trudging and driving through snow and ice to satisfy my many requests for local foods, and for taking me to places I might not have visited on my own. At the Crane Centre, thank you to Miyuki Kawase for sharing her time and knowledge. Thanks also to Ernest Mok and Ayaka Ōkawa for their assistance at Lake Akan.

In Teshikaga, many thanks go to Yukiko Kobayashi, Satoko Sugaya and Kylie Clark for arranging my meeting with Isori-san and Saitō-san and visit to Lake Kussharo, which turned out to be one of the highlights of my entire life. And to Kylie, I am grateful for your ongoing support of my work, whether it has been as part of Wondertrunk, Pantechnicon, or any of your other endeavours.

In Sapporo and Ishikari, thank you to Phoenix Scotney, Shinobu Takafuji and Yukihiko Ōyama for everything from interpretation to planning to transportation. In Abashiri, thank you to Hiromi Yamashita and Yūko Higuchi for assisting with local arrangements. And finally, thank you to Misaki Teraoka and Chizuko Yamaguchi from Wakkanai City and Kazuhito Takeguchi from Rishiri for your warm and enthusiastic welcome, and to Mia Takeshige for her guidance, interpretation and insights throughout the trip.

While this particular cookbook relied on the contributions of more people than usual, every cookbook is a collaboration. And I am grateful to have worked once again with so many of my favourite creative people. First of all, thank you to Kate Pollard, who had the courage to commission this way back in 2020. Since then, Kajal Mistry, Eila Purvis, Esme Curtis, Holly Arnold, Laura Edwards, Tamara Vos, Aya Nishimura, Jo Cowan, Matthew Hague, and Evi O and her studio team have all played hugely important roles in bringing this book to life. It means the world that all of you have approached this project with such enthusiasm and dedication. I also owe an enormous thanks to Yuki Serikawa and Emiko Pitman, who assisted with translation.

I also wish to thank Dr Anna Sulan Masing and Prof Morgan Pitelka, who both offered incredibly helpful advice in terms of how to approach research and writing on Ainu food and culture. As someone who is not familiar with the complicated topic of indigeneity, your insights were invaluable.

Last, but far from least, I must express my endless gratitude to my wife Laura, who looked after our kids while I was away (which is not a one-person job) and has always shown such support for my work even when it is a massive inconvenience to our family, which it often is. Laura, you are one of the reasons I fell in love with Hokkaido in the first place and I hope we can go back together soon.

And to Tig and Felix: thank you for being on (mostly) best behaviour while I was away, and for (mostly) keeping an open mind when I am recipe testing. In a few years we can all go to Hokkaido together and you can tell me what I got wrong!

AINU

アイヌ

FOOD

料理

 粟 の 穂

'THE TRUE LOCAL FOOD OF HOKKAIDO'

PERSPECTIVES ON AINU CUISINE

Despite the persistent myth of Japanese monoculturalism, in reality Japan is a nation of multiple cultures and subcultures, and currently at the forefront of movements to recognise Japan's marginalised and indigenous people are the Ainu. The Ainu migrated many centuries ago from northern Russia, to Sakhalin, the Kuril Islands and, of course, Hokkaido – or *Aynumosir* in the Ainu language, meaning 'land of humans'. The old Ainu worldview also specified *kamuy mosir* (land of gods), *pokna mosir* (underworld) and *sisam mosir* (neighbour's land)[3] – a far friendlier term for Honshu than what the Japanese used for Hokkaido at the time: *Ezogashima*, or 'barbarian island'.

The characterisation of the Ainu as 'barbarians' was used to justify the Meiji government's colonisation of Hokkaido and the destruction of Ainu culture. The euphemistically named Hokkaido Former Aborigines Protection Act of 1899 forced the Ainu off their land and banned their language, religion and customs.[4] Ainu lineages and traditions were obscured or lost completely over subsequent decades of assimilation and disenfranchisement. Logging and farming caused the extinction or endangerment of species that were important sources of traditional Ainu food and medicine. The number of Ainu language speakers dwindled from tens of thousands to just a few hundred.

But, Ainu culture survived – in homes, in enclaves based around former Ainu villages. Grassroots efforts to regain control over ancestral lands, counteract discrimination and assert the significance of Ainu culture began slowly in the 1920s and 1930s. These efforts gained momentum in the 1960s, which eventually resulted in a series of hard-won, long-overdue reforms.

In 1993, a legal case brought by Ainu landowners against the construction of a dam in Nibutani culminated in an official recognition that the Japanese government had taken land from the Ainu illegally. In 1997, the Ainu Cultural Promotion Act finally repealed the Former Aborigines Protection Act and marked a massive shift in the government's position, from denial and discrimination to promotion and preservation (at least in theory). In 2008, prompted by the UN's Declaration on Rights of Indigenous Peoples, the Japanese Diet adopted a resolution to officially recognise the Ainu as an indigenous group. However, the resolution was not actually written into law until 2019, as the Ainu Measures for Promotion Act.

While these new policies may have had symbolic significance, for many Ainu, they failed to deliver meaningful change. The 2019 Ainu Promotion Act was even condemned by the Ainu activist association Kotan no Kai,[5] whose president, Yūji Shimizu, stated: 'There are no clauses in the bill that guarantee aboriginal rights. The bill intends to use the Ainu people as a tourism resource, and we demand that the legislation be immediately retracted.'[6]

It can be difficult to disentangle the exploitation of the Ainu as a 'tourism resource' from sincere efforts to support their culture. In 2020, Upopoy, the National Ainu Museum and Park, opened in Shiraoi. This is a huge, impressive complex; a victory in terms of visibility and recognition. But it has also been criticised: for equivocating about the history of Ainu oppression, for retaining illegally obtained artefacts and remains,[7] and for drawing visitors away from smaller Ainu cultural centres, among other points of contention.[8,9,10]

Differing perspectives among the Ainu regarding efforts to assert their rights and culture are a reminder that Ainu society is not monolithic. In fact, the whole idea of 'Ainu society' is a little misleading; historically speaking, the Ainu were never organised as a single, united culture or centralised state, and geographically discrete Ainu settlements had divergent dialects and practices. Today, Ainu society is further complicated by how Ainu individuals identify – or don't identify – with their heritage.

During my research, I had the privilege of meeting and interviewing a few Ainu cooks, craftspeople and community organisers: Ryōko Tahara, an Ainu cookery instructor and organiser based in Sapporo; Hiromi Isori, a woodcarver living near Lake Kussharo, along with his wife Keiko Saitō; Akira Toko, a dancer, musician and craftsman from Lake Akan, who founded the Ainu art gallery-café Poronno in the 1970s; and his son-in-law, Yoshifuru Gōukon, who is not of Ainu descent, but now runs the café and has a comprehensive knowledge of Ainu food customs.

Throughout these interviews, some common threads emerged, such as reconciling old traditions with modern tastes, and a fundamendal ethos of honouring and serving the natural world. There was a recurring theme of preservation – of ingredients, identity, culture and the environment.

'We cannot create food unless nature creates it first ... We are given life by the blessings of the natural world.'

「自然界からものをいただかなければ、ものを作ったりができない。私たちは、自然界の恵みによって生かされている。」

RYŌKO TAHARA

I first met Ryōko Tahara at Pirka Kotan ('beautiful village'), an Ainu museum and cultural centre on the outskirts of Sapporo. Tahara is a lifelong Ainu cultural advocate, having been an official of the Sapporo Ainu Association, founder of the Ainu women's association Menoko Mosmos ('Women's Wake-Up'), and a representative of Ainu cuisine for Slow Food International. She also teaches cookery classes, which is the capacity in which I first met her.

For Tahara-san, cookery is an important way to communicate about the traditional Ainu worldview. 'Around 30 years ago, all Japanese people knew of Ainu culture was singing, dancing and woodcarving – but not food culture,' she says. 'I thought food was so important because it expresses the fundamental thinking behind the spirit of Ainu culture.' This is partially religious, Tahara says – hunting and fishing in particular are closely linked to the concept of kamuy (spirit-deities, pages 23 and 31) – 'But it's also done in consideration of the environment.'

Tahara continues, 'giving thanks to nature is the most important. We cannot create food unless nature creates it first.' She says this messaging is particularly prescient now, as we face the challenges of climate change. 'For some people,' she says, 'food can be how they start to consider nature,' starting with a simple recognition: 'we are given life by the blessings of the natural world.'

While Tahara-san dedicated herself to studying Ainu food before she began teaching others about it, it has always been a part of her life. She grew up in an Ainu family, in Mukawa, and learned to cook alongside her older sister when she was a child. Tahara explains that cooking was traditionally women's work, so women became important guardians of culinary culture after Meiji policies made it nearly impossible for Ainu people to forage, hunt or share food communally. Culinary traditions could only be maintained in private, domestic settings, mostly by women.

The cookbook-memoir *The Spirit of Huci* by Tomoko Keira explains the role of women in detail, especially with reference to the concept of summer as 'women's season' and winter as 'men's season':

> *The roles in the family were divided in those days. The tasks of working in the field and collecting and preserving wild vegetables are done by women, while hunting is for men ... After the Meiji era, deer hunting was prohibited as well as salmon fishing. Ainu men were restricted in what they could do in winter, but women kept working in summer.*[11]

And not only in summer – Ainu women kept working all the time, in home kitchens, keeping their families fed and their traditions alive over many decades of discrimination, just as they had over so many harsh Hokkaido winters.

In Tahara-san's family home, meals were a combination of Ainu and Japanese dishes, which were not always differentiated. As a child, she wasn't always aware of particular foods' Ainu roots, and Tahara-san references a number of dishes which could reasonably claim either Ainu or Japanese origins – such as *Sanpei-jiru* (page 53) and *cep ohaw* (page 34).

Tahara-san realised she could more easily parse what foods were traditionally Ainu by studying the language. 'We looked at the fish, the animals, the wild plants Ainu people were using – things that had Ainu names meant that they had been using them before people from Honshu arrived.' This highlights the importance of preserving the Ainu language, as well. Ainu has no written language, so the maintenance of traditions is absolutely vital. Historically, there were no Ainu 'recipes' – only verbal and physical transmissions, with an emphasis on movement,[12] which is also seen in other forms of Ainu art. 'We had to learn about Ainu cooking through experience,' Tahara says.

For the most part, Tahara's Ainu recipes don't deviate from tradition, as she wants to retain the dishes' connection to nature and spirituality. 'But on the other hand,' she says, 'I want to expand Ainu food, and sometimes this means making new changes. Ainu food culture is based on hunting and gathering, and some natural items have already disappeared, so we have to use alternative ingredients.' Tahara herself adds olive oil to *rataskep*, and miso and ginger to *citatap*. These flourishes may be untraditional, but they don't fundamentally change the dishes or divorce them from Ainu culture. And besides, they're just plain delicious – which is hugely important when it comes to getting people to engage with any kind of new cuisine.

'How do we define things like "tradition" or "culture"? Things that were invented 150 years ago become "traditional", but does that mean that things invented after that are "not traditional"?'

「伝統とか文化とかと言うものは、どう言う意味？例えば、150年前の実験であったものが、これが伝統になります。それ以降に変化したら、それ伝統じゃないの？」

YOSHIFURU GŌUKON

This is a point that comes up in my discussion with Akira Toko and Yoshifuru Gōukon at Lake Akan's Ainu Kotan. Gōukon is the Wajin (ethnic Japanese) owner-chef at Poronno, an Ainu restaurant that was established as a small café in 1978 by Toko-san, his father-in-law, inside his art gallery, originally called Chikisani Folk Crafts Shop. At first, they only served tea and coffee. But after a while, they began offering simple snacks: mainly *sito* with kombu sauce or salmon roe. Toko-san himself didn't initially know how to cook Ainu dishes, but his wife, Midori, who grew up among a large Ainu enclave in Urakawa and was raised on Ainu food, taught him how.

Toko kept the shop's focus on crafts until 2000, when he handed over the keys to Gōukon, newly married to his daughter Fukiko (who, incidentally, appears in Ainu Mosir (page 244) and performs Ainu music with her sister Emi under the stage names Kapiw and Apappo). 'Ainu cuisine is usually cooked by mums,' he says, so he enlisted his mother-in-law to teach him some dishes. His wife might have done it instead, but she had her hands full with a newborn baby at the time. At first, 'it was a simple menu,' he recalls – just an ohaw teishoku, either venison or salmon, which they still serve today (and I can personally attest is delicious).

Over the years, the menu has expanded to include a number of other traditional Ainu dishes, such as *mefun* (salted salmon kidneys) (page 77), preserved wild garlic (page 61) and *ruibe* (page 32). In a feature in *Brutus* magazine,[13] Gōukon says that the food at Poronno is inspired by the 'taste of grandma' – specifically Fukiko's grandma. But that doesn't necessarily mean it's old-fashioned. Far from it, Gōukon isn't afraid to riff on the classics, making food with a creative flair that suits his customers' tastes.

One such dish is the *potceemo* pizza, which repurposes the classic fermented potato cakes as a deliciously nutty, doughy-crispy crust. 'Potceemo is a very simple flavour, so it makes sense to use it as a pizza base. But I also wanted to serve things people would expect from a typical restaurant – that's why we introduced curry. We used venison, and it was delicious.' Gōukon also includes traditional Ainu seeds and spices in his curry, but he is quick to clarify that he wouldn't call the curry Ainu food.

'It's complicated,' he says. 'Some people would prefer to keep the old traditions, but others accept changes as long as the main elements stay the same ... How do we define things like "tradition" or "culture"? Things that were invented 150 years ago become "traditional", but does that mean that things invented after that are "not traditional"?'

Gōukon's perspective is that Ainu food has always been dynamic and open to change. He points out that carrots and potatoes, now *de rigueur* in a bowl of ohaw, would have been a new twist in the 1870s. And some traditional foods, he says, are simply improved by being open to new innovations. He cites potceemo as an example. 'Potceemo made the "traditional" way might be mixed with sand and other substances, and the smell was quite harsh.'

Of course, it's also a matter of taste, and nostalgia, Gōukon says. 'There's an old customer who sometimes says that he misses the traditional stinky potceemo his elderly neighbour used to make. But he still comes to us because not many places serve potceemo.' But there's a limit to how far food should deviate from tradition before it becomes something else, which Gōukon is mindful of. 'We are consciously trying to keep some aspects unchanged,' he says.

One of the key principles in Ainu food culture is to refrain from over-foraging, always leaving some of the plants behind so they can re-grow. There are spiritual and social aspects to this, but it's also just practical. If you find a patch of wild garlic and pull it all up by the roots, you're destroying a renewable source of food.

自然界

の恵み

A related practice, shared by many other indigenous cultures, is utilising every possible part of both plants and animals. When Toko-san was a young boy, his mother and uncle made a kind of fish sauce by chopping, salting and fermenting salmon milt, offal and gills. 'We put it on top of freshly cooked rice and ate it. I loved that,' he recalls with a fond smile. 'I was not so strong when I was little, but now, I never get a cold or get sick, as I ate that kind of food all the time. It made me stronger! The Ainu call salmon "kamuy cep" – "god fish" – and I understand why.'

Toko and Gōukon explain how a religious reverence for important food sources can be seen in Ainu ceremonies. These include the *asiri cep nomi*, which welcomes new salmon as they return to rivers, and *iomante*, which gives thanks for bear meat and fur, received as divine gifts as the bear is dispatched. Gōukon explains, 'when we go into the mountains to gather wild vegetables or cut trees, we perform a ceremony to thank the gods. We offer rice, tobacco or *inaw* [decorative wooden sticks] – these are things the kamuy are very happy to receive, so we offer them to take home as omiyage.'

Gōukon continues, 'There are old Ainu tales that say if you waste what the kamuy have brought you, you'll get divine punishment ... But it's not just about divine punishment, it's just the way it is.' In pre-modern times, the consequences of wasting food in a climate as severe as Hokkaido's would have been punishment enough.

'At first I watched my mother and father and did what they did, but then I wanted to make things more freely ... Everybody makes the brown bear eating salmon, but I wanted to carve what I liked.'

「父と母の創ったものを真似したものを作ったけれど、それが終わったらもう自分の好き勝手なものを創りたかった、自由にね。鮭を咥えた熊が普通のお土産だったけれど，好きなものを彫りたくなった。」

HIROMI ISORI

A lot has changed since the 1800s. Ainu lifestyles are no longer so immediately reliant on nature. But for many Ainu artisans, such as woodcarver Hiromi Isori, it's still a source of inspiration.

Isori has been carving since he was 10 years old; his mother and father were both woodcarvers as well. I ask him if he mostly keeps with tradition in his work, but he says the whole idea of 'traditional' wood carving is difficult to define, as historically the Ainu mostly carved wood to make tools, whereas now it is done mostly to make art or souvenirs. For him, it has always been a medium for creative expression.

'At first I watched my mother and father and did what they did, but then I wanted to make things more freely,' he says. 'Everybody makes the brown bear eating salmon' – one of the most ubiquitous motifs in Hokkaido folk art – 'but I wanted to carve something different.' His work is inspired by some of Hokkaido's most striking sights, such as white-tailed eagles or the Milky Way. Eventually, Isori did carve a few bear sculptures – but only after seeing one himself and understanding its form firsthand.

Isori's work is personal, but he is also moved by how it can create emotional connections to other people. He proudly recalls how a shop owner told him that one of his pieces brought a woman to tears when she saw it, and he appreciates how something he makes might be bought by someone at a souvenir shop, and then become their family's treasure. This is something he doesn't take for granted; a true craftsman, he is always trying to improve his work. 'Every time I make something, I think: this is the best one,' he says. 'But a year or so later, I think, this is terrible!'

Isori also works with antlers and glass, but mostly carves katsura wood, which he buys from a timber-yard in Akkeshi. Ideally, he says, he would use wood from local forests, but cutting trees himself remains illegal. 'When the Meiji government took measures to ban the Ainu lifestyle, from that time we couldn't enter the forest freely and cut the trees. Before that, the Ainu concept was that we could cut the tree to take just the amount we need – not too much.' Considering how much logging is done in Hokkaido, there is something absurd about how the Ainu are still not allowed to take small amounts of timber to make art. Isori-san jokes about secretly taking wood from protected forests, and wrestling with deer to steal their antlers. (He actually gets them from potato farmers, who collect them from their fields so they don't get caught in the harvesters.)

In addition to providing an outlet for individual expression, woodcarving and other forms of Ainu art are also a means for building community. In 2007, he and his wife Keiko Saitō opened Kussharo Factory, a communal space where Ainu woodworkers could come together to practise their craft and exchange ideas.

Most of Isori's experience with Ainu food also centred on communal gatherings, festivals and ceremonies such as iomante, where classic dishes like *cipor imo*, ohaw and rataskep would be served. But in his daily life, he tends to prefer Japanese food with a Hokkaido accent, which is what he grew up with – things like curry rice, nikujaga and Genghis Khan. He and Saitō appraise old-fashioned Ainu food as being a bit too plain for modern tastes. 'Back then we didn't have many seasonings,' Isori says. 'Just salt. Compared to how we eat now, the flavour seems wrong, too simple. Ainu nowadays prefer more seasoning.'

'Fifty years ago, there was no real interest in eating Ainu food,' Isori says. 'My mother might have cooked it, but she never told us, "this is traditional Ainu food" so I didn't know if we ate it or not.' However, he does remember helping his mother make one of his favourite Ainu dishes, potceemo, and he talks me through the process. 'Nowadays, potatoes are harvested by machine. But before, they were harvested by horse or by hand, and some of the potatoes would be left behind in the ground. They would then freeze underground, and thaw and freeze and thaw and freeze and thaw. So when spring comes around and the snow melts, the potatoes would have naturally fermented. I would pick the potatoes from the ground, and peel the skins, and then I would help washing and washing them to get the pure white starch.'

The laborious process is not something Isori has felt the need to persist with into adulthood. When I ask him if he cooks, he thinks for a moment, then replies with a chuckle: 'I boil ramen.'

Although Isori has no particular interest in food, even for him it is one way of maintaining connections within the Ainu community. He and Saitō are avid foragers; in their area they're able to find shiitake and maitake mushrooms, *sikerpe*, and wild alliums. 'I know where to find good wild garlic, and I helped Gōukon-san at Poronno source it.' Isori says. Saitō-san says that the Kussharo area has the best wild garlic, with a deeper flavour and stronger aroma.

Whether it's wood or wild plants, exchanging materials of cultural importance has always been a means of fostering community among the Ainu – and sharing knowledge on how to use those materials even more so. When she married Isori, Saitō-san was keen to learn Ainu embroidery; usually those kinds of skills would be passed down through families, but Isori's mother could not teach her as she was too old by the time they were married. Instead, Saitō learned from other people in the wider Ainu community, and she is now proficient enough to offer lessons to others, including people of Ainu descent. Isori notes that a renewed desire to learn about traditional crafts is connected to a broader trend of Ainu people feeling ready to reclaim their identity after so many decades of discrimination.

Interest in Ainu material culture is growing among non-Ainu people as well, which Isori and Saitō have mixed feelings about. A sincere desire to learn from another culture is a good thing, but sometimes people have only a superficial interest in Ainu culture, prompted by fashion or fiction. 'Now, even some Japanese people say, "I want to be Ainu!"' Isori laments. 'I try to tell them, no, no – it's very difficult!' Saitō-san explains, 'I guess they think it's cool, maybe because of *Golden Kamuy*' (page 49), and Isori agrees – people want Ainu stuff because they like how it looks, but that doesn't always translate to an understanding of Ainu culture. 'Some young people come here and they ask to buy inaw. But that's a spiritual thing,' he says. 'They're too influenced by the manga.'

ヒンナヒンナ

Tahara-san's grandmother was a traditional Ainu woman, with tattoos around her mouth and a sophisticated knowledge of wild plants that could be used for food and medicine. When Tahara was little, her grandmother would collect *seta-ento*, an herb in the mint family, and put it into porridge.

Tahara says the distinctive smell of seta-ento is very special to her – a sensory memento of her late grandmother. Taste and smell are unique among the senses in that they have a direct neural connection to our brain's memory centre. This is why food is so evocative, and can be a powerful way to remember and honour one's ancestors.

For decades, Ainu food has existed in mostly private spaces – in homes, or shared among Ainu communities. Now, it is becoming more public. Gōukon-san says he was initially nervous about presenting Ainu food to new people. 'There are people, even among the Ainu, who don't want to eat potceemo, don't like venison because of the way it smells, or don't want to eat wild vegetables because they have been eating them since they were children. So when we put up the signboard for our Ainu restaurant, I was honestly worried about whether it would be accepted by the world.'

But he says his fears have been allayed by the feedback he's received. 'I'm very happy with the reactions of my customers ... I'm happy to know that Ainu food culture, handed down from the past with no arrangements or modifications, is still accepted as wonderful even today.'

'We pick wild vegetables and ingredients ourselves, or ask our friends to get them for us – it's a way of thinking that people who have lived here for a long time have created in order to enjoy foods that have always existed in the land and seas of Hokkaido.' In this sense, he says, 'Ainu food is the true local food of Hokkaido.'

'When you enter an Ainu house, *cise*, you find sacred things, placed where you expect them to be placed. Everything is familiar to you, because of the information you have received through books or other sources. Now you think you know their story. This makes you think that you understand them and the context they are in. This in turn makes you very pleased. You found and understood what was expected. True, you understand more than people with no interest in those things, but you understand very little compared with us ... You are involved with theory, but you are not emotionally involved or tied to these things and you have no experience of how they work in practice. Therefore you see them as objects. As objects they have nothing living in them and they are what you call dead matter. To us they are both dead and alive ... Alive because they have something to tell us who understand how to interpret it properly, and dead to those who do not understand what is delivered. The message they hide from you, we can see clearly.'

1986 INTERVIEW WITH AN AINU COMMUNITY LEADER IN CHIKABUMI KOTAN,
CONDUCTED BY KATARINA SJÖBERG,
THE RETURN OF THE AINU [14]

阿寒湖アイヌコタン

ユクオハウ

AINU FOOD:
AN INTRODUCTION

INGREDIENTS, COMMON DISHES AND CONCEPTS

Historically, the Ainu are known to have eaten at least 500 different varieties of plants[15], not to mention dozens of land and sea animals. It is an enormously diverse cuisine. This book cannot provide a comprehensive guide to Ainu food, but hopefully it can at least act as a useful introduction. This overview and glossary is intended to clarify terms that are used elsewhere in this book, and to serve as a basic explanation of key Ainu dishes, ingredients and cultural ideas.

Ainu dishes are typically simmered, boiled, grilled, stir-fried or enjoyed raw. Food preservation is done mostly by drying, freezing or salting, and less frequently through fermentation. Common Japanese seasonings such as soy sauce, miso, sake and mirin were not part of pre-Meiji Ainu cookery, but modern Ainu food sometimes uses them. Ainu food is traditionally seasoned with salt, seawater, kombu and other seaweeds, and animal or fish fats, which are commonly substituted with vegetable oils in modern preparations. The Ainu have developed complex techniques for processing foods that would otherwise be inedible, such as detoxifying poisonous plants and isolating starch from roots and stems.

Ainu food culture is closely linked to spiritual ideas, namely the concept of kamuy – which can be described as gods, deities or spirits. (Some readers may note a similarity to *kami*, from Shintō, though it is not clear if they actually share a common cultural and etymological ancestor.) Generally they are understood as entities that exist within living things, and some non-living natural phenomena of particular power or importance. Thunder, snow, the undertow or even particular tools or machines may also be said to be or contain kamuy[16].

There are also kamuy that are responsible for the behaviour of animals collectively. For example, salmon are called kamuy cep – 'god fish' – and are revered in their own right, but they will also only come to fishermen who have venerated the *cepkorkamuy*, the god who summons salmon, or *cikapkamuy*, a great owl god who oversees and protects villages (*kotan*). Interestingly, not all animals are treated with the same regard – some Ainu traditions maintain that individual deer are not kamuy, but simply gifts from a more powerful god who controls them[17]. (Perhaps it is not a coincidence that *yuk*, the Ainu word for deer, also translates unceremoniously as 'prey'.[18])

Ainu religious traditions maintain many ceremonies and rituals that welcome kamuy when they arrive as food, and others that send kamuy off or release them when they are killed. As Ainu culture is highly regionalised, these practices and beliefs vary from place to place. The same can be said of Ainu dialects and, therefore, the names of many common foods. I have listed some of these variations below.

Much of the background information here comes from *Shizen no Megumi – Ainu no Gohan* by Hisakazu Fujimura, an invaluable field guide to the edible plants and animals of Hokkaido and their uses in Ainu cooking.

AHA アハ
VARIANTS: Eha, numinokan
JAPANESE: Yabumame, tsuchimame

Small beans that grow underground, recognisable by their shoots that appear when the snow melts. Modern iterations of Ainu dishes commonly use cultivated beans such as *toramame* or kidney beans instead.

AMAM アマム
VARIANT: Satamam
JAPANESE: Gohan, meshi, kokumotsu

Grains, including rice, barley and millet, the foundation of traditional Ainu meals.

CITATAP チタタプ
Finely chopped meat or fish, typically incorporating cartilage, small bones and offal, similar to a tartare or pâté. Usually eaten raw, but sometimes formed into meatballs and boiled in soup.

FIPE/RUIBE フィペ・ルイベ
JAPANESE: Sashimi

Fipe is simply food eaten raw, usually fish. Ruibe, which has become a popular preparation throughout Hokkaido, is sashimi served semi-frozen, but the Ainu word actually means 'thawed food'. It was historically a means of preservation rather than a way of serving.

HASKAP ハシカプ
VARIANT: Enumitanne

A type of honeysuckle which produces tart, blueish-purple berries, eaten as is, or used to flavour rice.

KAMUY CEP カムイチェプ
JAPANESE: Shake, sake

Salmon, perhaps the most important fish in Ainu gastronomy – hence the name 'god fish' or 'fish of gods'. It is prepared in a huge variety of ways: grilled, cooked in soup, dried (page 94), smoked and served raw, among many other methods. Salmon skin is also used to make waterproof boots.

KONPU コンブ
JAPANESE: Konbu

Kelp, commonly known by its Japanese name, kombu. There is evidence to suggest that the Ainu introduced kombu to Japanese gastronomy, though it may have arrived from China. In Ainu cuisine, konpu is eaten in soups, grilled or ground to a paste to make a sauce for sito.

MAKAYO マカヨ
VARIANTS: Makao, makayopo, pahakay, pakkay
JAPANESE: fukinotō

The giant butterbur is grilled, dried, or used in soups and simmered dishes after removing its alkaloid irritants through salting and boiling. Their enormous leaves are also said to provide shelter for a kind of gnome called *korpokkur*.

MAW マウ
VARIANTS: Otarop, otaroh
JAPANESE: Hamanasu

A variety of rosehips which grow near the coast, eaten fresh or dried. They are used to flavour soups, sauces or rice dishes (see recipe, page 42).

OHAW オハウ

Soups or thin stews, which form the basis for traditional meals, alongside a grain dish, usually based on meat or fish along with a mixture of vegetables, beans and wild herbs. Salmon and venison are the best-known varieties, but it can also use small birds, tanuki, sardines, herring and pork (see recipe, page 42).

POTCEEMO ポッチェエモ
VARIANTS: Peneimo, potceimo

Potatoes that are fermented through repeated freeze-thaw cycles over the course of the winter. They are then mashed and washed until only the clean starch remains, which is formed into a dough and made into pancake-like dumplings which are grilled or fried.

PUKUSA プクサ
VARIANT: Kito
JAPANESE: Gyōja ninniku

Wild alliums, sometimes called Alpine leek or pilgrim's garlic, which is one of the key flavourings in Ainu food. Traditionally it is dried for use throughout the year; nowadays it is also commonly pickled in soy sauce (page 60).

RATASKEP ラタシケプ

Translating as 'mixed things', this is a broad category of mashed dishes, typically vegetables, but also incorporating seafood or pulses (legumes). Classic examples include kabocha with beans (page 41), or potatoes with salmon roe.

SAYO サヨ
JAPANESE: Okayu

Porridge made from rice or millet, which may contain vegetables and/or herbs, often with medicinal properties. Along with ohaw, it is considered one of the cornerstones of Ainu meals.

SIKERPE シケレペ
VARIANTS: Sikerepe, seta-sikerpe
JAPANESE: Kihada

Berries of the Amur cork tree, with a bittersweet and highly aromatic flavour, similar to juniper or hops. A classic seasoning for rataskep, and now used in various creative preparations such as scones and gin.

SITO シト
Dumplings made from rice flour or similar starches such as potato, millet or pumpkin. Can be served plain but are often accompanied by a sauce; kombu, salmon roe and walnut (page 41) are common.

SUSAM スサム
JAPANESE: Shishamo

A small fish said to resemble a willow leaf, which is more important than salmon in some areas. Mukawa, for example, still holds a kamuy nomi (god welcoming) ceremony for susam at the beginning of their season.

TUREP トゥレプ
VARIANTS: Erapas, kiw
JAPANESE: Ōubayuri

The bulb and roots of the giant lily, which are processed to separate the starch from the fibre; both parts are then dried to be used in different preparations.

YUK ユㇰ
JAPANESE: Ezoshika

Ezo deer, one of the most important meats in Ainu cuisine, often cooked into soups but also smoked, dried or eaten raw.

SHIRAOI

白老

TUREPPON

MASCOT: TUREPPON

For Upopoy, TureppoN: a giant lily bulb (*turep*), who carries a *turepakam,* a disc of dried turep starch, and a turep stem with seed pods, which she scatters on the ground 'to grow new friends'. Upopoy's website explains the unusual capitalisation of Upopoy Mascot TureppoN name: 'In Japanese, cuteness is often indicated by adding an "n" to the end of a word. TureppoN's name has a capital N because she's VERY cute!'

ETYMOLOGY

From the Ainu *siraw o i*, 'place with many horseflies', or possibly *sirar o i*, 'place with many tides'. The kanji transliteration means 'white old man'.

POPULATION: 15,516

白老

S
H
I
R
A
O
I

白老

In 1881, the Emperor of Japan made a state visit to Shiraoi, on Hokkaido's southern coast. At that time, Shiraoi's population was 655 people, and 498 of them were Ainu. As explained in Ibrahim Jalal's *Hokkaido*, 'the nation building of the Meiji oligarchs involved publicising the Emperor's official visits across the nation, and reporting on [his] visit to Shiraoi made the town and its Ainu inhabitants known throughout the country.'[19] The Ainu townspeople performed a 'faux iomante' ceremony for the Emperor, and initiated what would become a long history of ethno-tourism in Shiraoi.

As the Japanese government disenfranchised the Ainu, and Wajin (ethnic Japanese) encroached upon their livelihoods – predominantly fishing and farming – the Ainu in Shiraoi increasingly turned to tourism as a 'business opportunity'. In the 1920s and 30s, more faux iomante ceremonies were held, and the local school was used as a venue for Ainu dance performances, open to the public.

By the mid-1960s, Shiraoi was attracting half a million visitors per year, to watch Ainu performances, listen to talks, and buy art and souvenirs sold in a reconstructed kotan.[20] In 1967, an Ainu railway porter and tour guide named Takeichi Moritake founded a small museum of Ainu culture, with the express purpose of correcting misconceptions about the Ainu. Over the years, the museum expanded to include restorations of Ainu cise (houses), *cip* (wooden boats), a botanical garden growing plants used in Ainu culture, and a café serving Ainu food. The museum ultimately housed over 5,000 Ainu objects and 7,500 books. They even obtained a licence to produce *tonoto*, a traditional Ainu liquor.[21]

Ultimately, the Shiraoi Ainu Museum's collection was incorporated into the National Ainu Museum and Park: Upopoy, which opened to great fanfare in 2020. Upopoy is built upon the same location as the former Ainu Museum, on the shores of Lake Poroto, with hot spring steam rising from the mountains in the distance. The surroundings provide an evocative environment in which to learn about Ainu culture.

In a way, it's impossible for any museum to avoid objectifying the people it represents. Museums display things (that's their job) and this is necessarily done at a distance from the viewer, creating a sense of separation – an othering, which is hard for any museum to overcome. But Upopoy challenges this dynamic in a number of ways.

白老

S
H
I
R
A
O
I

白老

→

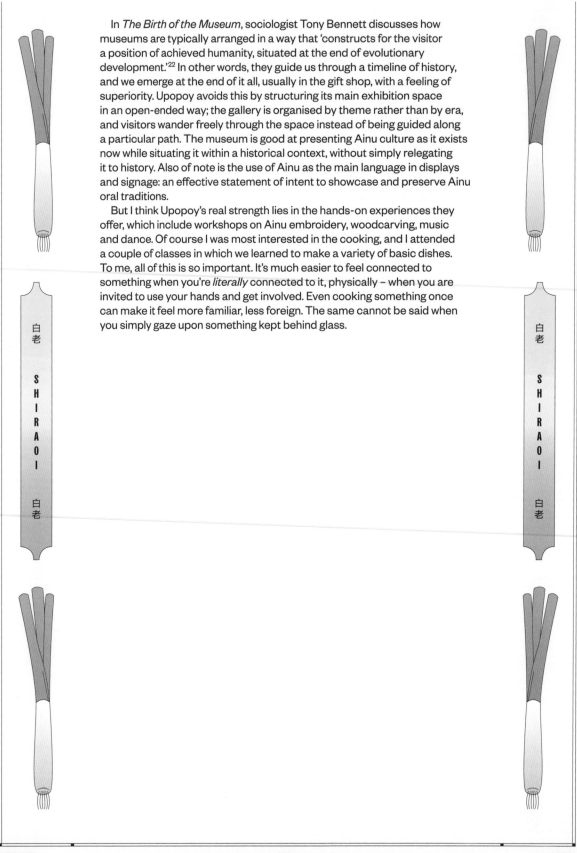

In *The Birth of the Museum*, sociologist Tony Bennett discusses how museums are typically arranged in a way that 'constructs for the visitor a position of achieved humanity, situated at the end of evolutionary development.'[22] In other words, they guide us through a timeline of history, and we emerge at the end of it all, usually in the gift shop, with a feeling of superiority. Upopoy avoids this by structuring its main exhibition space in an open-ended way; the gallery is organised by theme rather than by era, and visitors wander freely through the space instead of being guided along a particular path. The museum is good at presenting Ainu culture as it exists now while situating it within a historical context, without simply relegating it to history. Also of note is the use of Ainu as the main language in displays and signage: an effective statement of intent to showcase and preserve Ainu oral traditions.

But I think Upopoy's real strength lies in the hands-on experiences they offer, which include workshops on Ainu embroidery, woodcarving, music and dance. Of course I was most interested in the cooking, and I attended a couple of classes in which we learned to make a variety of basic dishes. To me, all of this is so important. It's much easier to feel connected to something when you're *literally* connected to it, physically – when you are invited to use your hands and get involved. Even cooking something once can make it feel more familiar, less foreign. The same cannot be said when you simply gaze upon something kept behind glass.

白老

S
H
I
R
A
O
I

白老

白老

S
H
I
R
A
O
I

白老

AYNU RECIPES

CONTRIBUTED BY CHEF HIROAKI KON

Hiroaki Kon was born in Sapporo in 1968. In 1987 he moved to Osaka to pursue a career as a chef, which led him to work in high-end kitchens in both Japan and Italy. In 1996, he opened his first restaurant in Honmachi, Osaka, which he would later rename 'kerapirka' (Aynu for 'delicious'), with a mission to serve and pass on the Aynu cuisine of his roots.

Kon-san returned to Sapporo in 2019, and reopened Kerapirka at its current location in 2020. He also began acting as a communicator about Aynu cuisine and providing catering for Aynu events and ceremonies, including Slow Food's Terra Madre festival in 2019. In 2021, Kon-san established Aynu Base, a company that works to promote not only Aynu food but other Aynu arts, with the goal of weaving traditional Aynu culture into the future. He also appears in a video display of Aynu artisans shown at Upopoy.

In 2021, Kon-san was selected for a research grant by the Aynu Folk Culture Foundation, which resulted in the publication of a book, *Aynu Food: Listening, Knowing, Making, Eating* (*Aynu no Shoku: Kiite Shitte Tsukutte Taberu* アイヌの食　聞いて知って作って食べる), a compilation of interviews with other people who have experience with Aynu food. In 2022 he was appointed as a member of the Committee for the Study of Aynu Cultural Assets, and in 2023, he was hired by the City of Sapporo as a consultant on Aynu food as well as an instructor of Aynu cookery in various venues.

Kon-san says: 'There is very little information about Aynu food in print, so I am planning to publish an Aynu cookbook based on my own experiences and interviews. We are currently accepting offers from interested publishers.'

For now, it is my privilege to present a few of his recipes in the pages that follow.

NOTE

Chef Kon prefers to use the phonetic romanisation 'Aynu' rather than the common Hepburn romanisation 'Ainu'. We have maintained this preference in the translations of his recipes and biography.

PUMPKIN MASH WITH BEANS, SWEETCORN AND SIKERPE

RATASKEP ラタシケプ

Kon-san says: rataskep means 'mixed things'. It can be made with many other ingredients, not just kabocha. Sikerpe are the berries of the kihada (Amur cork) tree, a broadleaf tree in the citrus family. They are used in Chinese herbal medicine, and also as a traditional medicine among the Aynu.

SERVES 4
50 g (1¾ oz/½ cup) dried sikerpe berries
150 g (5½ oz) dried beans, soaked in water overnight
    or for at least 8 hours – use a firm variety such
    as white kidney, pinto or calypso
500 g (1 lb 2 oz) kabocha, thinly sliced
130 g (4½ oz) corn kernels (cooked)
salt and vegetable oil, to taste

METHOD
Soak the sikerpe in enough water to cover while you prepare the rest of the dish. Boil the beans until soft, drain well and set aside. Boil the kabocha until soft, drain, then return to the pan and mash roughly, then stir in the cooked beans, corn and soaked sikerpe (discard the water). Season to taste with salt and oil.

RICE FLOUR DUMPLINGS WITH WALNUT SAUCE

NINUM (KURUMI) SITO ニヌム（胡桃）シト

Kon-san says: *ninum* are walnuts, and *sito* are dumplings. Apart from rice, sito can also contain *kibi* and *hie* (different types of millet) or frozen and thawed potato.

SERVES 4-5 (MAKES ABOUT 20 DUMPLINGS)
200 g (7 oz/1⅓ cups) Japanese rice flour
    (ideally komeko, but jōshinko is okay too)
just-boiled water, as needed (about 5 tbsp)
100 g (3½ oz/1 cup) walnuts
2 tbsp caster (superfine) sugar
½ tsp shōyu (or more, to taste)

METHOD
Mix the water into the flour, then knead until it forms a dry, smooth dough. Shape into flat, round circles, about 4 cm (1½ in) in diameter, with a slight depression in the middle. Boil the dumplings in plenty of water for about 5 minutes, then remove with a slotted spoon and transfer to a bowl of cold water. Gently rinse the dumplings in the water to remove the starch from their surface, then drain and place on a tray or plate.

Lightly toast the walnuts, then grind to a smooth paste with a mortar and pestle. Add the sugar and enough hot water to thin the paste into a thick sauce. Stir in the soy sauce, taste and adjust seasoning as needed. To serve, arrange the sito on a plate and spoon over the walnut sauce.

PORK KNUCKLE SOUP

PAIKA/PUTA OHAW パイカ・プタオハウ

ROSEHIP RICE

MAW AMAM/MAW GOHAN マウアマム・マウごはん

Kon-san says: Ohaw is soup, which can be made from many different things, such as meat, fish, vegetables and wild plants.

Puta means 'pig'; this recipe uses pork knuckle (*paika*).

SERVES 4

500 g (1 lb 2 oz) pork knuckle (raw, uncured)
2 litres (68 fl oz/8½ cups) water
1 garlic bulb, outer papery skin removed
   but bulb kept whole
about 50 g (1¾ oz) fresh ginger root,
   washed and thinly sliced (peel left on)
150 g (5½ oz) dried beans, soaked in water overnight
   or for at least 8 hours – use a firm variety such as
   white kidney, pinto or calypso
130 g (4½ oz) corn kernels
150 g (5½ oz/⅔ cup) pressed barley
salt, to taste

METHOD

Place the pork knuckle in a saucepan and cover with cool water. Bring to the boil, then rinse well under fresh water to remove scum and excess fat. Add the 2 litres (68 fl oz/8½ cups) water to the pan and add the garlic and ginger along with a little salt, and bring to the boil. Add the knuckle to the water, reduce the heat, and keep at a low simmer until the knuckle is soft and falling off the bone – about 3 hours. Boil the beans and corn separately, until cooked, then add them to the pork broth along with the pressed barley. Keep cooking for about 15 minutes, until the barley is cooked, then adjust seasoning as you like with salt.

Kon-san says: *Maw* is the Aynu word for *hamanasu* (rosehips). This recipe uses dried rosehips.

SERVES 4

3 tbsp (10 g/⅓ oz) dried rosehip shells
340 g (12 oz/1½ cups) rice (washed)
½ tsp salt
1 tbsp vegetable oil
450 ml (15¼ fl oz/scant 2 cups) water

METHOD

Combine all ingredients and cook according to the instructions on page 243.

NOTE

The barley called for here is oshimugi, or 'pressed' barley, which is different from pearl barley or rolled barley, neither of which will work. You can buy pressed barley at Korean supermarkets.

LAKE KUSSHARO

屈斜路湖

KUSSIE

MASCOT: KUSSIE
Unofficially – and mysteriously – 'Kussie', a reclusive lake monster, similar to that of Loch Ness.

POPULATION: 6,955 (TESHIKAGA TOWN)

ETYMOLOGY
Possibly from the Ainu *kutcaro,* for 'throat', describing the point where Lake Kussharo flows into the Kushiro River (see also: Kushiro, page 217).

汐ならぬ
久寿里の湖に　舟うけて
身も若がえる　こゝちこそすれ

It isn't the sea,

But when I take a boat out on Lake Kussharo,

I am young again.

TAKESHIRŌ MATSUURA[23]

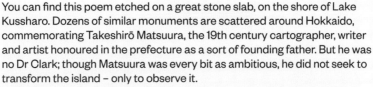

You can find this poem etched on a great stone slab, on the shore of Lake Kussharo. Dozens of similar monuments are scattered around Hokkaido, commemorating Takeshirō Matsuura, the 19th century cartographer, writer and artist honoured in the prefecture as a sort of founding father. But he was no Dr Clark; though Matsuura was every bit as ambitious, he did not seek to transform the island – only to observe it.

Matsuura worked closely with Ainu guides, learning their lay of the land as well as their language.[24] Even though he was from what is now Matsusaka, his love for Hokkaido was so great that he gave himself the pseudonym 'Hokkai Dōjin' – traveller of the north seas or, read another way: Hokkaido person.

Matsuura's poem expresses the beauty of Lake Kussharo far better than I ever could. To gaze out upon the glassy surface of Lake Kussharo is to have a moment of clarity.

Matsuura wrote this poem in 1858, when he was about 40 years old. His turn of phrase *mi mo waka gaeru* could be interpreted to mean 'even my body becomes young'. I think I know how he felt. Visiting Lake Kussharo made me feel younger because it made the world feel new again.

屈斜路湖 LAKE KUSSHARO 屈斜路湖

SIDES, SMALL DI

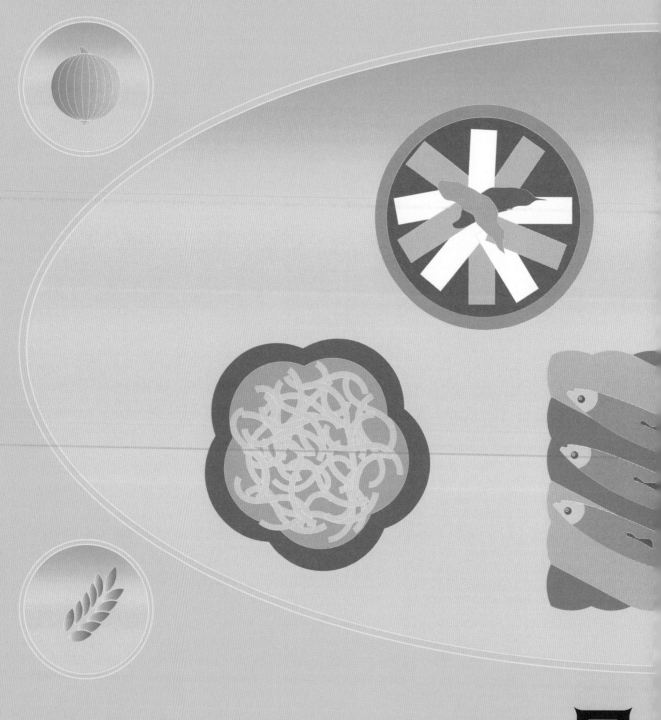

一品

SHES & SNACKS

料理

ABASHIRI

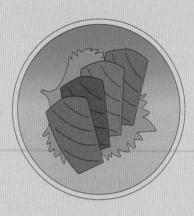

網走

NIPONE

MASCOT: NIPONE

Nipone, a genderless, flying creature who protects the city from monsters. Their form is a combination of traditional *nipopo* wood-carved dolls and the famous 'sea angel' gastropods (*clione*) which live beneath the drift ice in the Sea of Okhotsk. They wear an Ainu headband and an Ezo murasaki azalea, the official flower of Abashiri.

ETYMOLOGY

Ainu origin, possibly from *apa siri*, 'leaking ground', referring to an underground water source in a cave; *ci pa sir,* 'the land we discovered'; or *cipa sir*, 'island of offering'.

POPULATION: 33,004

© Abashiri City

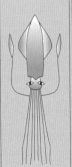

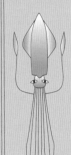

網走

A B A S H I R I

網走

War is everywhere you look in Hokkaido. Coastal cities built around former naval bases. Local specialities derived from wartime rationing. And the famous Abashiri Prison: established in part to house war criminals – particularly the 'last samurai' of the Satsuma domain, who rebelled against the government in 1877.

Abashiri Prison is also a key setting in the interwar thriller-heist manga *Golden Kamuy*, set in 1907 Hokkaido. At first, I had trouble getting into *Golden Kamuy*. It struck me as a kind of old-fashioned, gratuitously violent and gory Tarantino knockoff – *The Hateful Eight* crossed with *Inglourious Basterds* – but make it Hokkaido. (I'm really more of a *Jackie Brown* guy.)

But I returned to the manga after I learned about how much research author Satoru Noda had put into it, and how it has a level of historical detail rarely seen in period fiction. Noda worked closely with educators in order to faithfully depict elements of Ainu culture, and each volume has a works cited page – pretty serious scholarship for a manga.

There's also a wealth of information on food, accompanied by lovingly drawn, intricate illustrations. The way Noda depicts Meiji-era Ainu food in particular with such clarity is astonishing, and mouthwatering. For me personally, of course, all of this is enormously useful. But these depictions aren't just educational; food itself often drives the plot, establishes key themes and deepens character development through food-related memories and shared meals. In an article for *Vittles*, Kambole Campbell writes that 'there are moments in *Golden Kamuy* – even if it's just sharing miso and frying whale into tempura – which represent a kind of wish fulfilment of what could have been: a genuine exchange between cultures, rather than the erasure of one by the other.'[25]

Golden Kamuy may be a historical fantasy, but at its core, it's a war story, and a rousing one. The horrors of war are shown for what they are – gruesome and deeply traumatising – but they are also all part of the adventure, presented within an action-packed, swashbuckling, sometimes even comical context.

Then again, maybe Noda is more of a realist than an idealist. War is the story of Hokkaido, whether we want it to be or not. Abashiri Prison itself played a role in the military-industrial-agricultural complex, as well. Inmates were made to perform labour that supported the colonisation of Hokkaido put to work farming and processing food, partly for the prison's own self-sufficiency, but also to supply growing numbers of settlers on the island. Inmates were also given parcels of land after they had been trained and released, so they could continue to contribute towards the economic development of the empire.

Abashiri Prison was relocated to a modern facility in 1984. The original has been turned into a museum, preserving its original 'panopticon' layout, along with a range of agricultural artefacts housed within reconstructed barns

網走

A B A S H I R I

網走

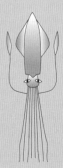

→

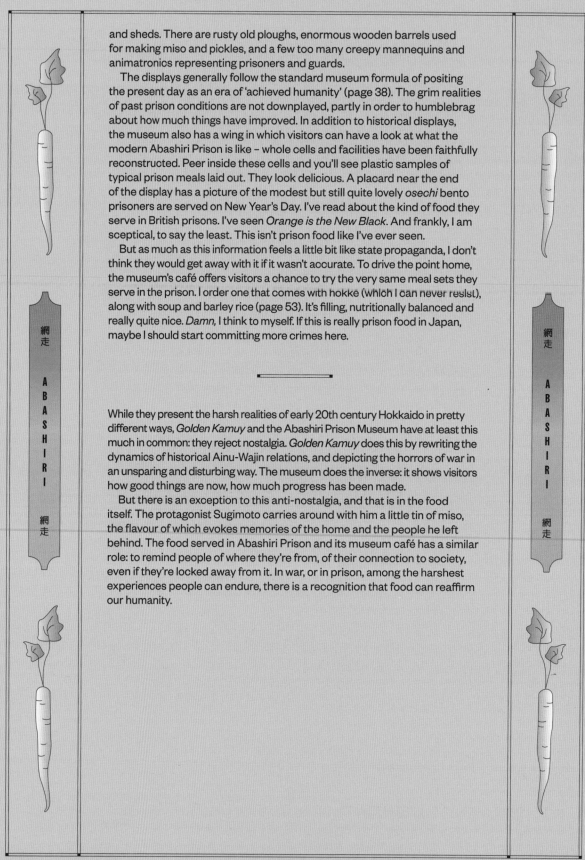

and sheds. There are rusty old ploughs, enormous wooden barrels used for making miso and pickles, and a few too many creepy mannequins and animatronics representing prisoners and guards.

The displays generally follow the standard museum formula of positing the present day as an era of 'achieved humanity' (page 38). The grim realities of past prison conditions are not downplayed, partly in order to humblebrag about how much things have improved. In addition to historical displays, the museum also has a wing in which visitors can have a look at what the modern Abashiri Prison is like – whole cells and facilities have been faithfully reconstructed. Peer inside these cells and you'll see plastic samples of typical prison meals laid out. They look delicious. A placard near the end of the display has a picture of the modest but still quite lovely *osechi* bento prisoners are served on New Year's Day. I've read about the kind of food they serve in British prisons. I've seen *Orange is the New Black*. And frankly, I am sceptical, to say the least. This isn't prison food like I've ever seen.

But as much as this information feels a little bit like state propaganda, I don't think they would get away with it if it wasn't accurate. To drive the point home, the museum's café offers visitors a chance to try the very same meal sets they serve in the prison. I order one that comes with hokke (which I can never resist), along with soup and barley rice (page 53). It's filling, nutritionally balanced and really quite nice. *Damn,* I think to myself. If this is really prison food in Japan, maybe I should start committing more crimes here.

———

While they present the harsh realities of early 20th century Hokkaido in pretty different ways, *Golden Kamuy* and the Abashiri Prison Museum have at least this much in common: they reject nostalgia. *Golden Kamuy* does this by rewriting the dynamics of historical Ainu-Wajin relations, and depicting the horrors of war in an unsparing and disturbing way. The museum does the inverse: it shows visitors how good things are now, how much progress has been made.

But there is an exception to this anti-nostalgia, and that is in the food itself. The protagonist Sugimoto carries around with him a little tin of miso, the flavour of which evokes memories of the home and the people he left behind. The food served in Abashiri Prison and its museum café has a similar role: to remind people of where they're from, of their connection to society, even if they're locked away from it. In war, or in prison, among the harshest experiences people can endure, there is a recognition that food can reaffirm our humanity.

網走

A
B
A
S
H
I
R
I

網走

おいしいまち

JAPANESE MEALS, HOKKAIDO STYLE

ABASHIRI PRISON BARLEY RICE

ABASHIRI KANGOKU NO MUGIMESH I 網走監獄の麦飯

Though Hokkaido's food culture is distinct from the rest of Japan, day-to-day meals are still focused on rice and side dishes. Plain white Japanese rice (page 243) will do, but this barley rice, served at the Abashiri Prison Museum and apparently in the actual prison itself, is a nice way to incorporate Hokkaido produce.

SERVES 3-4
250 g (9 oz/1⅛ cup) rice
50 g (1¾ oz/¼ cup) quick-cooking barley
   (such pressed barley or Italian pearl barley)
420 ml (14¼ fl oz/1¾ cups) water

METHOD
Combine the rice and barley and rinse well. Transfer to a saucepan or rice cooker and cook according to the instructions on page 243. Leave to rest for 10 minutes before serving.

SALMON AND VEGETABLE SOUP

SANPEI-JIRU 三平汁

Hokkaido produces excellent miso, and of course any soup made from this miso is delicious. However, meals in Hokkaido may also be served with fish-based soups, called Sanpei-jiru. Sanpei-jiru typically uses salt-cured salmon, which lightly seasons the broth, and can also be made with *ara*, the meaty trim of the fish. The origin of the name 'Sanpei' is debated, but one theory is that it is a corruption of the Ainu word *sampe*, which means 'heart', and may have referred to an Ainu soup made from salmon hearts and other offal.[26]

SERVES 4
800 ml (28 fl oz/3⅓ cups) Kombu Dashi
   (page 241, but from a powder is fine)
100 g (3½ oz) salmon ara (meaty salmon trim,
   spine bones, heads, etc.)
1 small potato (150–180 g/5½–6½ oz),
   cut into large chunks
1 carrot, peeled and cut into large, irregular wedges
100 g (3½ oz) daikon, peeled and cut into irregular wedges
3 tbsp sake
1 tsp caster (superfine) sugar
7.5 cm (3 in) baby leek, sliced at an angle
150 g (5½ oz) salt-cured salmon (page 138)
   or fresh salmon, cut into bite-size pieces
salt or miso, to taste

METHOD
Combine the dashi, salmon trim, potato, carrot and daikon in a saucepan and bring to a low boil. As it boils, remove the scum that forms on the surface of the broth. It will take about 10–15 minutes for all of the scum to come out of the salmon, at which point the vegetables will also be cooked. Add the sake, sugar, leek and salt-cured salmon and simmer gently for 2–3 minutes until the salmon is cooked through. Taste the broth and add salt or miso as needed.

VARIATIONS
Sanpei-jiru can be made with other fish, as well as crab (called *kani-jiru*). For this, use raw crab in its shell to make the broth, then pick the meat from the legs and claws to serve in the soup itself.

LAYERED VEGETABLE AND SALMON PICKLES

SAKE NO HASAMI-ZUKE 鮭のはさみ漬け

Hokkaido is home to a wide variety of unique pickles, many of which incorporate seafood, such as *su-ika* (squid pickled in vinegar), *shiokara* (salt-preserved offal) and *izushi* (salmon preserved in rice kōji). The cold temperatures of Hokkaido (or your refrigerator) help keep the seafood fresh as it cures. One such pickle which is relatively simple to make at home is *hasami-zuke*, made by layering vegetables with kōji and salmon, lightly fermented over a few days in the refrigerator. The result is a tangy, salty, umami pickle with literal layers of flavour and a striking, stratified appearance. The salmon for this should be pre-frozen in order to kill any potential pathogens or parasites.

MAKES ABOUT 12 PORTIONS

10 g (⅓ oz) kombu (one piece, about 8 × 16 cm/3 × 6 in)
2 tbsp rice vinegar
300 g (10½ oz) Chinese leaf (napa cabbage) – about 8 large, green outer leaves
1 carrot, peeled
150 g (5½ oz) daikon, peeled
100 ml (3½ fl oz/scant ½ cup) sake
6 sanshō peppercorns
½ small dried red chilli, cut into very fine rings
zest from 1 lime or ½ lemon, finely sliced or grated
15 g (½ oz) salt
100 g (3½ oz) shiokōji (paste, not liquid)
120 g (4¼ oz) very fresh (sashimi quality), smoked or salt-cured salmon (page 138), boneless, skinless and thinly sliced

METHOD

Place the kombu in a saucepan with 1 tbsp of the vinegar and enough water to cover, and leave to soak overnight. Set the pan over a medium heat, bring to a low boil and sustain for 20 minutes, then remove the kombu from the liquid, leave to cool, and cut it into two squares, each about 10 cm (4 in) across. Discard the liquid.

Microwave the cabbage leaves for 2–3 minutes to expel excess moisture. (Alternatively, they can be salted and then rinsed.) Squeeze out the wilted cabbage, then cut each leaf in half, widthways, so you have about 16 broad, roughly rectangular cabbage pieces.

Cut the carrot and daikon into thin planks, about 8–10 cm (3–4 in) long and 2–3 mm (⅛ in) thick. Bring the sake, sanshō and chilli to a low boil, then remove from the heat, add the citrus zest and remaining 1 tbsp vinegar, and stir in the salt until it dissolves. Leave to cool, then stir in the shiokōji.

Pack the vegetables and salmon into a container, ideally about 10 or 12 cm (4–4¾ in) square, in layers, following this pattern: cabbage, kōji brine, carrot, daikon, brine, kombu, brine, salmon, brine, daikon, carrot, brine, cabbage, and finish with the last of the brine. Press down firmly on the layers to expel any air pockets. Keep a weight on the pickles to keep them submerged in the brine, then ferment in the refrigerator for two to three days, and eat within 10 days.

KOMBU AND DRIED SQUID IN SWEET SOY SAUCE

MATSUMAE-ZUKE 松前漬け

This iconic pickle is so named for the Matsumae domain that dominated southern Hokkaido for the duration of the Edo period. The modern version, pickled in sweetened soy sauce rather than salt, was invented in 1937 by Masao Kaitō of the Yamagataya company, an innovation that turned it into one of Hokkaido's most popular preserves.

MAKES ABOUT 20 PORTIONS

25 g (1 oz) dried squid
25 g (1 oz) kombu
½ carrot, peeled and julienned
90 ml (3 fl oz/generous ⅓ cup) water
4 tbsp shōyu
4 tbsp mirin
2 tbsp sake
2 tbsp brown sugar
½ tsp katsuo dashi powder
1 cm (½ in) piece fresh ginger root,
    peeled and cut into fine shreds
½ dried red chilli, deseeded and thinly sliced
freshly grated horseradish, to taste (optional)

METHOD

The squid and kombu should both be cut into very thin shreds – no more than 3 mm (⅛ in) wide. You may be able to buy them like this, but if not, lightly dampen both the squid and kombu with a little water to make them more pliable before cutting with kitchen shears.

Place the kombu and squid shreds in a bowl along with the carrot. Combine all of the seasonings in a saucepan and bring to the boil, then pour over the kombu-squid-carrot mixture. Leave to soften and infuse for 2–3 hours, tossing the mixture a few times to ensure even marination. Pack into a container and leave in the refrigerator for two to three days, stirring every day, before eating. This will keep for about two weeks in the refrigerator. If you like, top with grated horseradish just before serving.

函館朝市

かけ 円	入船ぶっかけ 1500 円	松風ぶっかけ 1950 円	末広ぶっかけ 1620 円	若松ぶっかけ 1820 円	宝来ぶっかけ 2420 円

あわび大名盛 2530 円 — 大名盛 1800 円 — 根ホッケ定食 1580 円 — しまホッケ定食 1650 円

お好み4色 ぶっかけうに入り 2200 円 — お好み4色 ぶっかけ 1480 円 — いくらサーモン ぶっかけ 1500 円 — かにぶっかけ 1512 円

お好み3色 ぶっかけうに入り 1580 円 — お好み3色 ぶっかけ 1080 円 — 大名レディース 1280 円 — いくらぶっかけ 1980 円 — 生うにマグロ ぶっかけ 1980 円

定食 A 1180 円 — 定食 B — 活ホタテ刺 — ぎんだら定食

PRESERVING
WILD ALLIUMS

One of Hokkaido's most delicious plants is *gyōja ninniku*, literally 'pilgrim's garlic', but also known by its Ainu names *pukusa*, *kito* and *kitopiro*, as well as Ainu onion, Alpine leek or wild garlic. Though gyōja ninniku looks like European wild garlic (or American ramps), its flavour is more like a cross between wild garlic and three-cornered leek. Whichever you can find, you can preserve or pickle them in the same ways – by drying them or by packing them into soy sauce or miso.

WILD ALLIUM MISO

GYŌJA NINNIKU NO MISOZUKE 行者にんにくの味噌漬け

This exquisite and simple preserve is especially good with chargrilled meats but also tastes great simply dolloped onto rice.

MAKES ABOUT 200 G (7 OZ)
about 60 g (2 oz) wild garlic or wild leeks,
    washed and coarsely chopped
120 g (4¼ oz) miso (nothing too dark)
2 tbsp caster (superfine) sugar

METHOD
Mix all ingredients well, then pack into a container and press a piece of cling film (plastic wrap) directly onto the surface of the paste. Put a lid on the container and keep in the refrigerator; it will be ready to eat after a few weeks, and it will keep indefinitely.

WILD ALLIUMS PICKLED IN SOY SAUCE

GYŌJA NINNIKU NO SHŌYUZUKE 行者にんにくの醤油漬け

The slightly sweet, slightly spicy brine from this pickle makes a fantastic dip, and of course the salty chunks of wild garlic that come out of it are delicious in their own right. They are especially good with eggs, pork or tofu.

MAKES ABOUT 100 G (3½ OZ)
5 tbsp shōyu
1 tbsp mirin
1 tbsp sake
½ tsp sesame seeds
¼ tsp sesame oil
1 dried chilli
40 g (1½ oz) wild garlic or wild leeks,
    washed and coarsely chopped

METHOD
Combine all of the seasonings in a saucepan and bring to the boil, then leave to cool for a few minutes, pour over the chopped alliums and mix well. Leave to cool, then pack into a jar and lay a piece of cling film (plastic wrap) directly onto the surface of the brine. Put a lid on the container and keep in the refrigerator; it will be ready to eat after a few hours, but it is much better after a few weeks, and it will keep indefinitely.

MICROWAVE-DRIED WILD ALLIUMS

RENJI DE KANSÔ SHITA GYÔJA NINNIKU レンジで乾燥した行者にんにく

Dried wild garlic is used throughout the year in Ainu cookery to add a subtle allium flavour and umami boost to dishes such as ohaw (page 42) and sayo. I initially tried to dry my wild leeks the traditional way: in the sunlit, windswept air. I did not consider that these adjectives do not describe the air in London, so my leeks didn't so much dry as wither, turning yellow and flaccid.

Enter the microwave, which has the unique effect of expelling moisture from foods by boiling the water within it. It preserves both colour and flavour better than oven-drying (which is fine, too, but also not as quick). But watch out for scorching – once a piece of allium has lost its moisture, the microwaves will get to work on other molecules within the leaves, causing them to burn. Err on the side of caution with cook times and power levels.

This method is for a 800W microwave – adjust cook times accordingly for your wattage.

METHOD

Take a handful of wild alliums and lay them out on a plate, in between two pieces of paper towel. Cook on full power for 1 minute, then shuffle the leaves around, and continue to cook in 30 second bursts until they are mostly dry. If the paper towel becomes damp during this process, replace it with fresh sheets.

Turn the microwave down to half power and continue cooking, 30 seconds at a time, until the leaves are totally dry. Remove the paper towels and leave to cool, then place into a container lined with a cloth or more paper towel and store in a dark, dry place.

WILD ALLIUM GYOZA

GYŌJA NINNIKU IRI GYŌZA 行者ニンニク入り餃子

Wild alliums make an outstanding addition to gyoza. I have personally had these at both Teshikaga Ramen and Ichiryūan in Sapporo, and can attest they are an ideal accompaniment to ramen.

You can use either wild garlic or wild leeks for these, or a mix of both. Out of season, *nira* (garlic chives) are the best substitute. This recipe calls for shop-bought gyoza wrappers, but feel free to make them from scratch.

MAKES 40 GYOZA

FILLING
500 g (1 lb 2 oz) fatty, coarse minced (ground) pork
100 g (3½ oz) wild garlic or wild leeks, finely chopped
1 leaf of Chinese leaf (napa cabbage), finely chopped
2 fresh shiitake mushrooms, destemmed and
    finely chopped
¼ tsp salt
¼ tsp MSG
¼ tsp ground white pepper

TO ASSEMBLE AND COOK
40 gyoza wrappers
water, as needed
cornflour, for dusting
about 1 tbsp oil
shōyu, vinegar and chilli or sesame oil, to taste

METHOD
To make the filling, mix everything together by hand until all of the vegetables are well-distributed throughout the pork. Don't mix more than you have to, as this can make the filling dense and pasty.

Use a small spoon to portion the filling into the centre of each wrapper. Dip your fingertips in water and dampen the edge of each wrapper, then fold the wrapper over the filling, pressing firmly along edges to seal. (Pleat if you like; gyoza are served upside-down so it doesn't actually matter that much.) As you make them, line the gyoza up in neat rows on trays lined with parchment and lightly dusted with cornflour.

To cook, heat a spoonful of oil in a non-stick pan or, better yet, a very well-seasoned cast-iron pan, over a medium-high heat. Add the gyoza, sealed side up, and fry until the bottoms are golden brown – about 3–5 minutes. Without turning the gyoza, add about 100 ml (3½ fl oz/ scant ½ cup) of water to the pan and put the lid on. Steam for 5 minutes.

Remove the lid and let the remaining water evaporate from the pan to ensure crisp bottoms. When they're done, carefully lift them from the pan with a spatula, or turn them out directly onto a plate. Serve with soy sauce, vinegar and a few drops of chilli or sesame oil on the side for dipping.

生蟹

恋愛

YOUNG LOVE
AND FRESH CRAB

We were in Sapporo for Laura's birthday, 2007. We checked into the New Otani Hotel and asked the concierge if he could recommend a good local crab restaurant; he suggested Kani Honke, a Sapporo-based chain known for the enormous animatronic crabs that loom over their frontages (a feature shamelessly lifted from Kani Honke's Osaka-based competitor, Kani Dōraku).

We arrived at the restaurant and ordered a bottle of sake and one of the set menus. This included crab shūmai, rich dark crab meat grilled in the shell, and a selection of *kani zukuri*: legs of various types of crab that had been boiled, chilled and neatly sliced open so we could easily pull out long, satisfying chunks of the sweet, cold meat within. The meal was light; we left sated but buoyant, and more than a little bit tipsy. But back then, a little bit tipsy was never tipsy enough. So we went to a bar – a bar of my choosing, for some reason, even though it was Laura's birthday. I selfishly chose Beer Inn Mugishutei, Sapporo's original craft beer bar, run by an American named Phred Kaufman who is such a bear of a man it's become a cliché to describe him as a bear of a man.

When we visited, Phred's phridges held more than 250 beers – an incredible selection for Japan at that time. Needless to say, I left staggeringly, stupidly, prize-winningly drunk. Somewhere along the walk back to the hotel, I professed to Laura that I thought I could marry her. This wasn't just the alcohol talking – I was just ridiculously happy and full of crab and madly in love, and the beer just made it that much easier to tell Laura how I felt.

I was mortified when she reminded me what I'd said the next morning, with a hangover that felt like that giant crab from Kani Honke digging its spiky claws into my skull. I tried to retract my declaration, but you know what they say: you should either do what you say you'll do when you're drunk, or quit drinking. Reader, I did not quit drinking.

This is all to say that a dinner of Hokkaido crab, accompanied by plenty of sake and followed by heroic quantities of high-strength craft beer is – apparently – a recipe for romance. So enjoy the crab recipe that follows, drink lots of imperial stout, then send me a thank-you postcard from your honeymoon.

CRAB GRILLED IN ITS SHELL

KANI NO KÔRA YAKI かにの甲羅焼き

This recipe uses a whole, medium-sized crab. Here in the UK, this is most likely to be a brown crab, but you can also get spider crab, which is more similar to what you'd get in Hokkaido. Either will work.

SERVES 2, OR UP TO 4 AS PART OF A LARGER MEAL

1 whole crab, about 1 kg (2 lb 4 oz), fresh or frozen
1 tbsp shōyu
1 tbsp white miso
1 tbsp sake
1 tbsp mirin
1 tsp prepared wasabi
10 g (⅓ oz) butter (optional)
a few chives, finely sliced
¼ lemon

METHOD

If you've purchased a live crab, kill it quickly: lift up the triangular flap towards the back of the abdomen, and drive a metal skewer or thin knife deep into the smooth but distinct depression underneath. This will destroy the crab's central ganglia and kill it within seconds. (If you have purchased a frozen crab, it will already be dead, of course, and you can skip this step.) Bring a large pot of water to the boil and lower in the crab. Cook for 15 minutes, then remove and leave to cool.

Remove the legs from the crab. Crack open the legs and claws, and pull the meat out in solid chunks. Use a chopstick or small skewer to pick out any white meat from the base of the shell where the legs were attached.

Pull off the abdominal shell of the crab, and remove and discard the feathery gills. Scoop out the brown meat, and coarsely chop any large, firm chunks. Combine the brown meat with the little bits of white meat from the base of the shell, along with the soy sauce, miso, sake, mirin and wasabi, and mix well. Rinse out the shell and dry it, then scoop the dark meat mixture back into the shell. Place on a tray under a hot grill (broiler) and cook until bubbling and browned, then top with the picked leg and claw meat and the knob of butter (if using), then return to the grill for just a minute to warm the meat through and melt the butter. Garnish with the chives on top and the lemon wedge on the side.

FLAVOURED BUTTERS

The butter in Hokkaido needs no embellishment, but why not gild the lily by blending it with complementary seasonings? These are a few of my favourites you might come across in Hokkaido cooking. Soy sauce and miso with butter are pretty common, versatile combinations; the lavender butter is admittedly a bit more niche. I had it on potatoes at Farm Tomita – a perfect combination – but I have suggested other uses on the following pages.

SOY SAUCE BUTTER

SHŌYU BATĀ 醤油バター

MAKES ABOUT 100 G (3½ OZ) - ENOUGH FOR 2-4 DIFFERENT DISHES
75 g (2½ oz) unsalted butter, very soft
  (a tiny bit melty is good)
2 tbsp shōyu

METHOD
Whisk the soy sauce into the softened butter,
little by little, until fully incorporated and smooth.

APPLICATIONS
Melt onto sweetcorn, scallops, potatoes, steak, cabbage
or noodles. Or basically anything.

MISO GARLIC BUTTER

NINNIKU MISO BATĀ にんにく味噌バター

MAKES ABOUT 100 G (3½ OZ) - ENOUGH FOR 2-4 DIFFERENT DISHES
50 g (1¾ oz) miso
50 g (1¾ oz) unsalted butter, softened
1 garlic clove, grated (optional)

METHOD
Smash the miso and butter together (along with
the garlic, if using) until smooth.

APPLICATIONS
Delicious on any grilled seafood, especially scallops,
prawns (shrimp) or white fish; also great with lamb, corn,
asparagus or rice.

LAVENDER BUTTER

RABENDĀ BATĀ ラベンダーバター

MAKES ABOUT 100 G (3¹/₂ OZ) - ENOUGH FOR 2-4 DIFFERENT DISHES
100 g (3½ oz) salted butter
1 tbsp lavender buds
oil-based lavender food colouring, as needed (optional)

METHOD
Place half of the butter in a saucepan with the lavender and set over a low heat. Melt the butter and let the lavender infuse for 10 minutes, keeping the heat low so the butter doesn't brown. Pass the melted butter through a sieve and stir back into the remaining butter, along with enough food colouring to turn it pale purple. Chill in the refrigerator until set.

APPLICATIONS
Melt onto potatoes, with plenty of sea salt, or use to baste roast lamb or chicken. Also delicious lightly spread onto toast with honey.

RICE-STUFFED SQUID

IKAMESHI イカめし

Like so many great dishes, ikameshi was a product of ingenuity during a time of hardship. In 1941, rice was scarce due to wartime rationing, so folks had to find other ways to bulk out their meals. At that time in Uchiura Bay, there was a surplus of squid, and so the proprietors of Abe Bento Shop at Mori Station tipped the typical balance of a bento towards protein, taking a generous amount of squid and filling it with a relatively small amount of rice. Mori was a hub for rail traffic carrying soldiers to northern bases, and the innovative bento quickly became well-known among troops.

Word spread throughout the country about Mori's exquisite ikameshi, and today it remains one of Japan's most iconic ekiben. It's a perennial favourite in the *furusato nōzei* tax redistribution scheme, which allows people living in Japan to divert a portion of their taxes to the municipality of their choosing in exchange for gifts of produce from that area. Ikameshi has even been sold in America, at the Japanese supermarket Mitsuwa, making it one of very few ekiben that can be called internationally famous.

SERVES 2

180 g (6⅓ oz) mochi rice (*mochigome*)
400 g (14 oz) squid, cleaned
1 cm (½ in) fresh ginger root, washed and thinly sliced
450 ml (15¼ fl oz/scant 2 cups) dashi
3 tbsp shōyu
3 tbsp sake
3 tbsp caster (superfine) sugar
1 tbsp mirin
water, as needed

METHOD

Wash the rice, then cover with water and soak for 1 hour. Meanwhile, if your squid has tentacles, chop them into pieces no longer than 1 cm (½ in). Drain the rice through a sieve. Divide the rice evenly into the squid tubes along with the chopped tentacles, if using. Weave a toothpick through the squid tube openings to close them.

Place the ginger in a saucepan, then add the squid, side by side (don't pile them up), along with the dashi and all of the seasonings. Top up with water to barely cover the squid, then top with a cartouche, and bring to the boil. Place a lid on the pan, reduce the heat to low and leave to simmer for 45 minutes. Remove the lid, turn the squid over and increase heat to high and cook for another 10–15 minutes until the liquid has reduced to a thin sauce. In the final 5 minutes of cooking, turn the squid frequently to coat all sides in the sauce. Remove from heat and leave to cool in the sauce for at least 15 minutes. Discard the ginger before serving. These will be tender enough to just eat with chopsticks, but if you like, they can also be sliced into rounds with a sharp knife.

POTATO CHEESE DUMPLINGS

CHĪZU IMOMOCHI チーズいももち

In potato-packed Hokkaido, there is a type of mochi that uses mashed potato and starch in place of glutinous rice. They are aptly called *imomochi*: potato mochi. The basic version is quite plain, but I have seen many variations on them including cheese, honey, soy sauce and butter; this recipe uses all of the above.

**MAKES 8 MOCHI (ABOUT 3-4 SERVINGS –
THEY'RE NOT VERY BIG, BUT QUITE DENSE AND FILLING)**

80 g (2¾ oz) mozzarella or similar mild melty cheese, or 4 Babybels (see method)
400 g (14 oz) potatoes (peeled weight)
4 tbsp potato starch or cornflour (cornstarch)
100 ml (3½ fl oz/scant ½ cup) milk
¼ tsp salt
2 tbsp vegetable oil, plus a little more, for greasing your hands
20 g (¾ oz) butter, divided into 4 or 5 little pieces
2 tbsp honey
3 tbsp shōyu

METHOD

Cut the cheese into eight little slices, about 2.5 cm (1 in) wide and 5 mm (¼ in) thick – Babybels are perfect for this; just cut them in half across the middle to make two thin circles. Cut the potatoes into 2.5 cm (1 in) chunks, place in a microwave-safe bowl and cover with cling film (plastic wrap) and microwave on full power (800W) for 5–6 minutes until soft. (You can boil them as well, but make sure they don't become waterlogged.) Mash the potatoes along with the starch, milk and salt until smooth – the mixture should be fairly dry and clay-like.

Divide the mixture into eight equal portions, rub your hands with a little bit of vegetable oil, and shape each piece of dough into a ball. Flatten each ball and place a piece of cheese into the centre, then wrap the potato dough around the cheese to enclose it. Heat the oil in a non-stick pan over a medium-high heat and fry the dumplings for about 4 minutes on each side until browned. Blot any excess oil from the pan with paper towel, then reduce the heat on the pan to low and drop in the butter in small pieces all around the pan. Drizzle over the honey and soy sauce and keep cooking for a few minutes until it forms a sticky glaze, gently turning the dumplings a few times to coat them evenly. Remove from the heat and leave to cool for a few minutes before serving.

ISHIKARI

石狩

SAKE-TARO & SAKE-KO

MASCOT: SAKETARŌ & SAKEKO
Saketarō and Sakeko, a boy and girl dressed as salmon who can communicate in both Japanese and 'sakana-go' (fish language). Their tops bear the initials of docosahexaenoic acid and eicosapentaenoic acid – two omega-3 fatty acids found in abundance in Ishikari salmon.

ETYMOLOGY
Several possible Ainu origins, including *isikar a pet* (circulating river) and *isikari* (obstruction), perhaps referring to bends in the Ishikari River that make it difficult to see upstream.

POPULATION: 57,756

Some foods that are named after the place that's famous for them are tremendously disappointing. (I'm looking at you, New York pizza and hot dogs.) As you might imagine, this disappointment rarely occurs in Hokkaido, where local foods tend to live up to or even surpass their reputation. Yūbari melon is easily the sweetest, most succulent melon I've ever eaten. Rishiri kombu, a treasure from the depths. And of course, you can get damn good Ishikari nabe in Ishikari.

Ishikari nabe is said to have been invented by one restaurant, Kindaitei, which was founded in 1880 by a woman from Niigata named Saka Ishiguro. Amazingly, the restaurant is still operating today at its original premises, and has stayed in the family, now run by her great-granddaughter, Seiko Ishiguro.

Kindaitei occupies one of those old Meiji-era wooden buildings that feels a bit off-kilter – because it is. A century and a half of strong winds and heavy snowfall have made Kindaitei's ceilings bend, floors slant and walls tilt. It's probably a fun challenge to navigate if you've had a few drinks. There are antiques and mementos everywhere; with a little organisation, it could function as a museum. An ancient, wall-mounted box telephone hangs near the entrance, with the original phone number displayed beneath it: eleven. Just eleven.

I don't know what the original menu was back in 1880, but it feels like it probably hasn't changed much. It showcases nose-to-tail fin salmon cookery, utilising as much of the fish as possible. The famous hotpot is made mainly from ara – bones and trim. There is a pâté made from the liver and stomach, and preparations of roe and milt. The crunchy cartilage from the head is mixed with vinegared vegetables for a refreshing sunomono. It is a masterclass in the art of salmon parts.

There's also mefun, salted salmon kidneys. This is a type of shiokara (salt-preserved seafood offal) derived from Ainu cookery. Its flavour is very intense – only a tablespoon or so is served. Though I suppose this is also because a salmon only has so many kidneys.

People in Japan often ask me if there are any foods I don't like, or can't eat. I usually say mefun, or shiokara more generally. But I always hesitate when I do. I might not particularly like it now. But saying it that way feels like I'm ruling out the possibility that I could get better at it – that I could learn how to like it. Acquiring tastes is one of life's great joys. Besides, Kindaitei has been going for over 140 years – clearly, the problem is me, not the mefun.

NORI-WRAPPED SALMON BELLY
ISO NO KAORI 磯の香り

At Kindaitei (page 77), this simple preparation is called *iso no kaori*, or the 'scent of the seaside'. Upon frying, the nori and the salmon skin fuse and become one, crispy shell, which ruptures and releases a flood of juicy fish fat when you bite into it.

SERVES 2-4

200 g (7 oz) salmon belly (this is about what you'll get from one whole salmon), boned, scaled and cut into six pieces
salt, as needed
1 sheet of nori, cut into six rectangles
oil, as needed for shallow-frying

METHOD

Salt the salmon belly liberally; this is served with no sauce or dip so all of the seasoning will come from the salt. Wrap each piece of belly in a rectangle of nori, using a little water, if needed, to moisten and seal the nori. Heat a thin layer of oil in a non-stick or well-seasoned cast iron pan over a medium-high heat, then fry the salmon for about 4 minutes on both sides, until the nori and skin are crisp and the flesh is browned. Season with a little more salt and enjoy.

SWEETCORN TEMPURA FRITTERS

TŌMOROKOSHI NO KAGIAGE とうもろこしのかき揚げ

There are two key things that make this recipe great, both of which I learned from trying the superlative version served at the friendly Furano izakaya Gyoro Gyoro. First: use the sweetest, freshest corn you can (so that means save it for corn season, if you can resist). And second: there should be very little batter – just enough to coat and bind the corn. It's okay if a few loose kernels break free, so don't be tempted to add more batter or to thicken it beyond what the recipe calls for.

SERVES 4

600 g (1 lb 5 oz) fresh corn kernels (from 4 cobs)
20 g (¾ oz) cornflour (cornstarch)
55 g (1¾ oz/scant ½ cup) flour
about 1.5 litres (52 fl oz/6¼ cups) oil, for deep frying
40 g (1½ oz) sparkling water
good-quality sea salt or pink Himalayan salt, to serve

METHOD

Combine the corn and flours in a bowl, and mix well. Heat the oil in a wide, deep pan to 180°C (350°F), then mix the sparkling water into the corn, to form a batter. Use two spoons to slide scoops of the battered corn into the oil. Crowding the pan can result in soft batter, so cook in batches. When the kakiage are golden brown, lift each one out with a slotted spoon or chopsticks, and drain on a wire rack. Eat hot and fresh, sprinkled with plenty of salt.

RICE HOT DOG
HOMAGE TO JUN-DOG

JUN-DOGGU FŪ SŌSĒJI ONIGIRI ジュンドッグ風ソーセージおにぎり

The delightful speciality known as 'Jun Dog' – a sort of hot dog-onigiri hybrid – was originally invented by the restaurant Junpei, in Biei. However, it is now mostly associated with Asahikawa, where it has been made at Jirō Watanabe's café, Pijon Kan, for over 30 years.[27] It is also sold as a takeaway (takeout) item at various venues across the city, including the Asahiyama Zoo, Asahikawa Station and several hospital canteens.

MAKES 4 JUN-DOGS
240 g (8½ oz/1⅛ cup) rice
4 small-ish, smoky pork hot dogs (10–13 cm (4–5 in) long, about 60–70 g (2–2½ oz) each)

METHOD
Cook the rice according to the instructions on page 243. Boil or grill (broil) the hot dogs until done. Cut a square of cling film (plastic wrap) and lay it onto the counter or a cutting board, then scoop a roughly hot dog bun-sized pile of rice into the centre of the cling film. Lay a cooked sausage on top of the rice, and use the cling film to wrap the rice around the hot dog, squeezing it into a tubular shape once it's all wrapped up. Unwrap the rice-hot dog log onto a square of parchment, then roll it up into a tidy parcel, folding in the sides as you go. Enjoy warm and fresh, or chill in the refrigerator and reheat later. This can be done by microwaving the dog, still wrapped in paper, for about 30 seconds per dog.

VARIATION

These can also be made with ebi-fry (panko-coated prawns/shrimp). Top with a little tonkatsu sauce before wrapping in the rice.

A HOKKAIDO
CHEESEBOARD

HOMAGES TO FROMAGES

Hokkaido is home to over one hundred independent cheesemakers –
40% of the total number in Japan.[28] As Japan had no pre-modern cheese
traditions of its own, Hokkaido cheeses are based on styles from across
Europe, but most exciting to me are the unique Hokkaido cheeses
that incorporate local flavours not found in other countries. It's relatively
easy to recreate some of these at home, to make a cheese board with
a distinctly Hokkaido flavour.

Each recipe will be enough for 1–2 people, so if you make all of them
the cheeseboard will serve up to 8.

HORSERADISH SMOKED CHEESE
HOMAGE TO WA-CHIZU

YAMAWASABI SUMŌKU CHĪZU
山わさびスモークチーズ（和ちいずのオマージュ）

100 g (3½ oz) smoked Cheddar, cubed
1 tbsp strong horseradish cream

METHOD
Toss the Cheddar with the horseradish cream.
Cover and keep in the refrigerator for at least 4 hours,
and up to two weeks.

WINE CHEDDAR
HOMAGE TO FURANO CHEESE KŌBŌ

WAIN CHEDĀ
ワインチェダー（富良野チーズ工房のオマージュ）

100 g (3½ oz) medium or mature Cheddar, cubed
2 tbsp red wine
½ tsp red wine vinegar
½ tsp caster (superfine) sugar

METHOD
Toss the Cheddar with the remaining ingredients.
Cover and keep in the refrigerator for at least 8 hours,
and up to a week.

MISO BOCCONCINI
HOMAGE TO TAMURAYA

BOKKONCHĪNI MISOZUKE
ボッコンチーニ味噌漬け（たむらやのオマージュ）

1½ tbsp miso (any kind)
1 tbsp hon-mirin
1 tsp vinegar (any kind – balsamic is nice)
a pinch of chilli (hot pepper) flakes
a pinch of freshly grated citrus zest (optional)
100 g (3½ oz) bocconcini (drained weight)

METHOD
Stir together everything except the cheese until no
lumps of miso remain. Toss the bocconcini through
the miso marinade. Cover and keep in the refrigerator
for at least 8 hours, and up to a week.

YUZU KOSHŌ CHEESE
HOMAGE TO ARAKAWA BOKUJŌ

CHĪZU NO YUZU KOSHŌ AE
チーズの柚子胡椒和え（あらかわ牧場のオマージュ）

100 g (3½ oz) Manchego or similar, rind removed
1 tbsp yuzu koshō
1 tsp olive oil
½ tsp apple cider vinegar

METHOD
Toss the cheese with the yuzu koshō, olive oil and
vinegar. Cover and keep in the refrigerator overnight,
and up to two weeks. Slice before serving.

CROQUETTES

Hokkaido is korokke country – perhaps a natural consequence of the prefecture's many potato and dairy farms. They're not just delicious but also quite versatile, good alongside curry (page 119) or as a topping for burgers (page 126) or noodles (page 172).

Once you've made and shaped the filling, all of the korokke recipes that follow are assembled and cooked the same way. Dip them in the pané batter using a slotted spoon, toss in panko until well coated, then lift them out of the panko and place on a tray until ready to fry. It is much better to fry these when they are freshly made. You can freeze them, but they should be defrosted before frying.

Fry korokke at 170°C (340°F). For cream korokke it is important to be precise, so use a thermometer for this. If the oil is too hot it will boil the liquid inside too rapidly, bursting through the crust before it hardens. Too low, and the crust won't set and colour quickly enough. Use a large pan, with plenty of oil – it needs to be deep enough to completely submerge the korokke. I advise cooking no more than four at a time. Take them out when they're just golden brown – the longer they fry, the more pressurised they become, causing them to burst. As long as the oil is kept at 170°C (340°F) they should only need about 3–4 minutes. Drain on paper towel and rest for a few minutes before serving.

All of these korokke, except the squid ink and Camembert, should be served with plenty of tonkatsu sauce. The squid ink croquettes are nice with a squeeze of lemon.

十勝平野

PANÉ BATTER

MAKES ENOUGH FOR UP TO 8 LARGE OR 16 SMALL CROQUETTES
3 eggs
50 ml (1¾ fl oz/3½ tbsp) water
100 g (3½ oz/generous ¾ cup) plain (all-purpose) flour
1 tsp oil

METHOD
Whisk everything together until smooth.

MEAT AND POTATO CROQUETTES

KOROKKE コロッケ

Classic potato-based korokke are big in Hokkaido – sometimes literally. What better use for an abundance of potatoes, meat and onions? The inclusion of miso, garlic and ginger are not typical, and can be omitted, but I love how these seasonings mimic the flavour of Sapporo ramen, in a crispy-fried format.

MAKES 8 BIG KOROKKE, OR 16 LITTLE ONES
600 g (1 lb 5 oz) potatoes (unpeeled weight), peeled and cut into large chunks
2 tbsp butter
1 onion, diced
1 garlic clove, finely chopped
2 or 3 coin-sized slices of fresh ginger root, peeled and finely chopped
150 g (5½ oz) minced (ground) beef
3 leaves sweetheart (hispi) cabbage, finely chopped
2 tbsp sweetcorn (optional)
black or white pepper, to taste
2 tbsp miso
2 tbsp caster (superfine) sugar
¼ tsp salt, plus more as needed
1 batch pané batter (opposite)
about 120 g (4¼ oz) panko

METHOD
Boil the potatoes in sea-salty water until totally soft. Drain well and leave to cool and air-dry. Melt the butter in a pan over a medium heat and add the onion, garlic, ginger, minced beef, cabbage and corn (if using), and cook, stirring often, just until the meat is cooked through and beginning to brown. Stir in the pepper, miso, sugar and ¼ tsp salt, then remove from the heat, combine everything with the potatoes, and mash well. It's okay if they are a little chunky – but not too much, or they will be awkward to shape. Taste the mixture and adjust seasoning with salt and pepper, as you like. Chill the potato mixture in the refrigerator, then divide into 8 or 16 patties. Proceed to pané and fry as per the instructions on page 89.

CREAM CROQUETTES, THREE WAYS

KURIĪMU KOROKKE NO SANSHU クリームコロッケの種

Cream korokke, which are béchamel- rather than potato-based, come in two main varieties: kani (crab) and corn.

I have included a third, non-traditional variation here, which is flavoured with squid ink and Camembert cheese. This an homage to Furano Cheese Factory, a way of recreating the flavour of their signature 'Sepia', a Camembert-style cheese made with squid ink for a striking charcoal colour and deep umami flavour.

MAKES 10-12 CROQUETTES - ENOUGH FOR 4-6 SERVINGS
35 g (1¼ oz) butter
1 banana shallot, finely chopped
50 g (1¾ oz/scant ½ cup) plain (all-purpose) flour
¼ tsp salt (or more, to taste)
a few grinds of black pepper
a tiny pinch of chilli powder
200 ml (7 fl oz/scant 1 cup) milk
1½ tbsp double (heavy) cream
1½ tbsp sour cream
1 batch pané batter (page 91)
about 100 g (3½ oz) panko

METHOD
Place the butter and shallot in a large microwave-safe bowl and cook on full power (800W), uncovered, for 2 minutes. Whisk in the flour, salt, pepper and chilli, then add the milk, cream and sour cream, little by little, until fully incorporated, with no lumps of flour. Microwave again for 2 minutes, then whisk thoroughly and scrape down the sides of the bowl. Continue cooking in 1-minute intervals, whisking well after each one, until the mixture boils and becomes very thick.

Proceed to add additional ingredients, as per the instructions below, before panéing and frying.

Once the filling is complete, transfer to the refrigerator to chill completely. Oil your hands and shape the filling into oblong croquettes, then proceed to shape and fry them per the instructions on page 89. If you have followed the cooking instructions on page 89 and the korokke are still bursting, they can be reinforced by rolling the filling in panko before dipping in the pané batter, and then the outer coating of panko.

VARIATIONS

CRAB: once the béchamel is cooked, stir in 100 g (3½ oz) cooked crabmeat - any kind will do, including fake crab, but if you use dark meat, it should only be a small portion of the total amount so it is not too rich.

CORN: add 75 g (2½ oz) corn kernels to the bechamel. Cook them in the sauce for a few minutes, purée with a stick blender until smooth, then add another 75 g (2½ oz) whole (cooked) kernels, and stir them through.

SQUID INK AND CAMEMBERT: add 1 tsp squid ink and 50 g (1¾ oz) Camembert (including the rind) to the béchamel while still hot, and blend with a stick blender until smooth.

KOMBU-WRAPPED MACKEREL

SABA NO KONBUMAKI 鯖の昆布巻き

In Hokkaido, kombu is eaten in a number of Ainu and Japanese preparations, including *konbumaki*. These are simply batons of seafood – typically oily fish, shellfish or roe – wrapped up in kombu and braised in a sweet soy sauce. They are rich, sweet and dense with umami – perfect with warm rice or as part of a bento.

MAKES 18 BITE-SIZE PIECES

3 large squares (about 20 × 20 cm/8 × 8 in each)
    of kombu
1 litre (34 fl oz/4¼ cups) water
4 tbsp caster (superfine) sugar
4 tbsp shōyu
4 tbsp mirin
3 tbsp sake
2 tbsp vinegar
about 180 cm (71 in) of kanpyō (dried gourd strips),
    rinsed and soaked in fresh water for 10 minutes,
    and cut into 18 pieces
2 fresh mackerel fillets, boneless, cut into 12 goujons,
    each about 1 cm (½ in) thick and 8 cm (3 in) long

METHOD

Soak the kombu in the water overnight, then slowly bring it to the boil over a medium heat. Add all of the seasonings and cook at a low boil with a drop-lid or a cartouche on top for 30 minutes, then add the kanpyō to the liquid and cook for a further 30 minutes, until the kombu is tender and pliable. Remove the kombu and the kanpyō from the dashi and leave to cool.

Cut the kombu into six rectangular strips, each about 10 cm (4 in) wide. Roll two pieces of mackerel up in each strip of kombu, and secure each roll by tying with three strips of kanpyō (alternatively, you can secure them with toothpicks). Return the six rolls to the pan with the seasoned dashi, re-cover with parchment or a drop-lid, and boil for another 20–25 minutes until completely soft, letting the liquid reduce as it cooks. Remove from heat and cool in the cooking liquid before cutting each of the six rolls into bite-size pieces.

SALMON JERKY

SAKETOBA 鮭とば

Saketoba is enjoyed these days as a popular snack, but it began as an important way of preserving salmon. There is a similar Ainu preparation called *tupa* from which modern saketoba is probably derived. Modern versions are flavoured with soy sauce and sugar for a deliciously teriyaki-ish flavour. The kanji characters sometimes used to write this dish are a poetic evocation of their traditional production process: *toba* 冬葉, meaning 'winter leaves', as the fish were hung on wooden frames, rustling as they dried in the winter wind.

MAKES ENOUGH TO SERVE 2–4 AS A LITTLE SNACK

200 g (7 oz) salmon loin, skin on, boneless and scaled
4 g (⅛ oz) salt
3 tbsp shōyu
2 tbsp mirin
⅛ tsp dashi powder

METHOD

Cut the salmon, against the grain of the flesh, into long, thin strips, about 5 mm (¼ in) thick. Cover them with the salt, then leave to cure overnight. The next day, rinse and dry the salmon, then marinate in the remaining seasonings for 4 hours. Transfer to a rack and dry in a dehydrator or oven set to 70°C (158°F) for 12–16 hours, until the salmon is dark and glossy and very dry. Once dried, this will keep at room temperature for about a week.

MURORAN

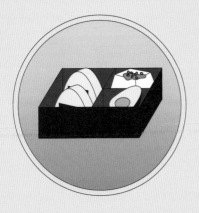

室蘭

KUJIRAN

© Muroran City

MASCOT: KUJIRAN

Kujiran, a whale whose blue colour represents the sea that surrounds Muroran. Kujiran is also typically depicted balancing a soccer ball atop a spout of water coming from his blowhole, in honour of Muroran's champion high school football teams, the many pro footballers who were born in Muroran and the local sports complex.

POPULATION: 76,841

ETYMOLOGY

From the Ainu *mo ruerani*, 'small slope', a phrase often truncated to *mo ruran*. Muroran is a hilly city and has many slopes, but the particular slope for which the city is named is located near Sakimori Station, in the far west side of the city. The slope currently has a three star rating on Google maps, with one review offering the appraisal: 'It's just a hill.'

室蘭

MURORAN

室蘭

室蘭

MURORAN

室蘭

Forget about Osaka. If you really want to kuidaore, Muroran is where it's at.

My visit began with ramen, as it often does, at Aji no Daiō (page 167), followed by Bokoi meshi (page 183), then yakitori (page 98) along with grilled pork cheeks, crab cream croquettes the size of Twinkies and an order of zangi which turned out to be half a chicken. Big, fat, Hokkaido portions.

I ate every last morsel served to me, because too much is never enough. Because there is so much to try and I can't bear to miss an opportunity to try it. And because I don't want the chefs to think I didn't love and appreciate what they'd cooked.

I left Muroran feeling ravaged by overindulgence, but also astonished at just how much great food this mid-sized city had to offer.

I grew up in a similar kind of place in Wisconsin: a post-industrial, coastal town with a declining population. In Muroran, the bus stops are named after factories; my hometown has high schools named after industrialists who made tractors and malted milk and furniture polish. Our food is not the same, of course, but it is similarly designed to use what's around, to put meat on your bones, and to cost very little.

I used to look back at my hometown with a kind of haughty disdain: a drive-through town in a flyover state, with nothing to offer. I feel differently now, with so many years and so many miles between me and the food I grew up with. During a layover in Tokyo I met a woman at a sushi bar who turned out to be from Hokkaido. When I told her I was going there to study local foods, she was surprised – she didn't think of Hokkaido as a place of having local foods worth studying.

They say familiarity breeds contempt. But more than that, it breeds indifference. I guess it takes a new perspective to change that. From the windows of a local bus, Muroran is just another run-down, overcast city. But at night, from the mountains, it becomes a starscape of factory lights; from London, it becomes a fond memory. Reality turns to romance. The mundane becomes mesmerising. Things look different, more fascinating, through a telescope or a microscope.

GRILLED PORK AND ONION SKEWERS

MURORAN YAKITORI 室蘭やきとり

Yakitori is chicken. It's in the name: 'yaki' is grilled, and 'tori' is bird. So yakitori is grilled bird. Except ... sometimes it isn't?

In Muroran, the word 'yakitori' refers specifically to pork. This odd misnomer came about in the 1930s, when a restaurant in Muroran called Toriyoshi began selling pork skewers alongside their standard offering of sparrows and small game birds.[29] At the time, there was a surplus of cheap pork in Hokkaido, a by-product of making leather for army boots required for the Sino-Japanese War. The pork skewers quickly outsold the original bird-based menu, and other shops followed suit. Ever since, in Muroran, yakitori has been made with pork instead of chicken, with an addictively sweet sauce and a thwack of hot mustard on the side. I cannot overstate how important it is to cook this over charcoal, so save it for a day when you feel like busting out the barbecue.

MAKES 16 SKEWERS

500 g (1 lb 2 oz) pork belly, shoulder
   or other fatty cut, rind off, frozen
1 onion
sake, as needed
salt and MSG, as needed
about ½ batch (90 ml/3 fl oz/generous ⅓ cup)
   Pork Tare (page 243)
Japanese *karashi* mustard or hot English mustard,
   as needed

METHOD

Take the pork out of the freezer about an hour before you need to prep it, perhaps a little less than that if your kitchen is quite warm. Using a sharp knife, cut the semi-thawed pork into strips about 5 mm (¼ in) thick, then cut the strips into chunks about 2.5 cm (1 in) square. You should get about 50–60 chunks total. Cut the onion into little petals, about 1 cm (½ in) wide and 2.5 cm (1 in) across. Working quickly, before the pork thaws completely, thread the pork onto 12–15 cm (4¾–6 in) long bamboo skewers, alternating each piece with one or two petals of onion. You will get 4 pieces of pork and 3–4 pieces of onion onto each skewer. Sprinkle the skewers with a little bit of sake, salt and MSG. (They will be further seasoned with tare, so don't use too much.)

Cook the skewers over charcoal until nicely charred on both sides. When each skewer is done, dip them in the tare, then return to the grill for a minute to caramelise. Serve immediately, with hot mustard on the side.

LAKE AKAN

阿寒湖

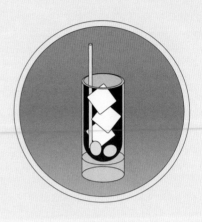

MARIMU

© Akan Tourism Association

MASCOT: MARIMU
Marimu, an anthropomorphic marimo dressed in Ainu clothing.

POPULATION: 6,518 (AKAN TOWN)

ETYMOLOGY
Various theories, originating in Ainu. Possibly from *akan*, meaning 'unmoving', referring to Mt Meakan and Mt Oakan, which held their form and position during a powerful earthquake centuries ago.

阿寒湖

L A K E A K A N

阿寒湖

Lake Akan is one of several picturesque lakes within Akan National Park; home to the Lake Akan Ainu Kotan, an area dedicated to the promotion of Ainu culture and business.[30] The kotan features a plaza of Ainu-run shops, including Poronno, one of Hokkaido's few Ainu restaurants (page 21), as well as community organisations that support educational and cultural events – most famously, the Marimo Festival.

Marimo are balls of algae that live in Lake Akan, which are extraordinarily popular as an attraction, mostly due to their kawaii appearance. They are soft, green and fluffy, drifting benignly beneath the waves like adorable little critters. They are often sold as 'pets', and referred to as 'lake goblins' (*torasampe*) in Ainu.

The festival is held in October, featuring Ainu performances and ceremonies with the express purpose of paying respect to the marimo as kamuy. Professor Jon Pitt refers to this as an instance of 'fakelore' because the marimo were not deified prior to the mid-20th century.[31] Their mythical status appears to be mostly derived from 'The Legend of Marimo Love', a made-up Ainu folktale written by Wajin author Kōsaku Nagata in his 1922 book *Mountain Legends and Love Stories*.[32] The tale involves two star-crossed lovers who commit suicide by jumping into Lake Akan, turn into marimo and live happily ever after. The story was further popularised by the enka song *Marimo no Uta*, recorded in 1953 by Mariko Andō.[33]

Meanwhile, marimo were designated a protected species, but regardless of this status, their numbers in Lake Akan declined throughout the first half of the 20th century, due to pollution, harvesting for souvenirs and the construction of a hydroelectric dam.[34] The marimo population became a metric by which the environmental health of the entire lake was measured, and the local Ainu community rallied behind the lil green guys as a symbol of their efforts to protect their homeland. Hence, the Marimo Festival was born, turning the fuzzy balls into both a spiritual entity and a symbol of indigenous environmentalism.

The festival has been criticised for inventing a new tradition based on a lie told by a Wajin writer, but the response to such criticisms has typically been along the lines of 'who cares?' Traditions gotta start somewhere, so why not in the waters of Lake Akan, where the marimo may bounce and sway with the gentle currents, forever and ever.

Marimo are not edible, but this hasn't stopped people from making foods in their image. There are marimo-inspired, matcha-flavoured mochi as well as marimo ramen, garnished with a bundle of edible seaweed that vaguely resembles the real thing. And there are apple-flavoured, spherical marimo jellies, delicious in their own right and even better in a 'Marimojito', a delightful cocktail served at local izakaya Ajishin – so you can have your marimo, and drink it, too.

WHITEBAIT TEMPURA
WAKASAGI NO TEMPURA わかさぎの天ぷら

Hokkaido's freshwater lakes and rivers are full of tasty things to eat. Among the most popular are *wakasagi*, little smelts that can be fried whole into tempura. But first, you have to catch 'em appraisal. Tourists can have a go at ice fishing for wakasagi on both Lake Akan and Lake Abashiri when they freeze over. I tried my hand at it, and caught a grand total of one after waiting patiently by my little ice hole for 45 minutes. When I took it back to the shack to be fried, the lady working there told me it was 'too sad' to fry just one, so she graciously gave me some she'd caught earlier.

The wakasagi were mild and sweet; some of them were filled with pockets of buttery golden roe. I think it's safe to say I'll never be a champion at fishing for wakasagi – but I'm *very* good at eating them.

SERVES 2, GENEROUSLY

150 g (5½ oz/⅔ cup) cold water (sparkling if you've got it)
1 egg white
100 g (3½ oz/generous ¾ cup) plain (all-purpose) flour
20 g (¾ oz) cornflour (cornstarch)
250 g (9 oz) whitebait
oil, for deep frying
lots of salt

METHOD

Whisk together the water and egg white, then stir in the flour and cornflour to form a thin, slightly lumpy batter. Heat the oil to 180°C (350°F), then dredge the whitebait in the batter, and fry in batches after letting the excess batter drip off. When the fish are golden and crisp, drain on paper towel and season generously with fine salt.
(I was admonished for asking if you might have this with *tentsuyu* or mayo, but I won't tell anyone in Akan or Abashiri if you wish to do so.)

RARE VENISON STEAK

SHIKANIKU NO REA SUTĒKI 鹿肉のレアステーキ

Historically, *Ezoshika* meat was the domain of Ainu cuisine, but it is now being incorporated into Japanese and yōshoku preparations such as Genghis Khan, *nikuman* and curry rice. It is also common to find venison steaks, served rare with a simple sauce, on izakaya menus.

SERVES 1-2

200 g (7 oz) venison steak
oil, salt and pepper, as needed
a knob of butter
1 garlic clove, unpeeled
2 tbsp red wine
2 tbsp apple juice
1 tbsp shōyu
1 tbsp caster (superfine) sugar

METHOD

Rub the venison with oil, salt and pepper. Heat a frying pan over a high heat until smoking hot, then lay the steak in the pan and cook for about 5 minutes, turning the steak (every 30 seconds or so) so that it cooks and browns evenly. In the final minute of cooking, add the butter and garlic to the pan and baste the venison in the butter as it melts.

Remove the steak, then add all of the remaining ingredients to the pan. Boil rapidly and reduce by half as the venison rests. To serve, slice the venison, and pour over the sauce.

セイコーマートの恵み

BLESSINGS
OF SEICOMART

The word 'blessings' (*megumi*) is used a lot in Hokkaido, on restaurant menus and travel brochures and supermarket displays and souvenir stands and hotel buffets; there's even a dog food brand called 'Blessings of Hokkaido'.[35] Basically, it turns up on any product or advertisement singing the praises of premium local produce – praises which, it must be said, deserve to be sung.

But some blessings of Hokkaido are more mundane – such as Seicomart, a locally-owned conbini chain. Of course, any conbini is a blessing – always there for you, for whatever you need. But Seicomart goes the extra mile, often literally, delivering quality food to remote areas where other shops are scarce. I've heard stories of Seicomarts being the only place in some towns to buy fresh produce, and of how they have sustained people stuck on Rishiri Island when storms have cancelled ferries for days.

But perhaps the most Hokkaido thing about Seicomart is its 'Hot Chef' counter. All conbini have hot food, of course, but Seicomart has made it a key feature, beckoning customers in from the bitter cold. Among my favourites of the Hot Chef range is warm onigiri, larger than average and filled with bacon *okaka*. A copycat recipe follows, along with something a bit lighter, but still with a distinctively Hokkaido character: a ham and cucumber sandwich, spiked with *yamawasabi* (horseradish).

HOT BACON OKAKA ONIGIRI

ATATAKAI BĒKON OKAKA ONIGIRI 温かいベーコンおかかおにぎり

MAKES 4 BIG ONIGIRI

4 slices of streaky bacon, cut into lardons
spent kezuribushi from making Kezuribushi (Dried Fish)
   Dashi (from 15 g (½ oz) dry kezuribushi, page 242),
   squeezed dry and coarsely chopped
2 tbsp dark brown sugar
1 tbsp shōyu
1 tbsp sake
water, as needed
1 tsp toasted sesame seeds (optional)
1 tbsp mayonnaise
4 portions of warm cooked rice
   (from 300 g (10½ oz/1½ cups) uncooked)
2 sheets of nori, cut in half

METHOD

Cook the lardons in a pan set over a medium-high heat for about 5 minutes, stirring often, until lightly browned. Tip in the chopped kezuribushi, sugar, soy sauce and sake, and add enough water to barely cover. Increase the heat to high and bring to the boil, then continue to cook for about 10 minutes, stirring often, until almost all of the liquid has evaporated. Switch off the heat and stir in the sesame seeds, leave to cool, then stir in the mayonnaise.

To make the onigiri, cut a square of cling film (plastic wrap) and lay it out on the counter, then lay out a half-sheet of nori on top of the cling film. Scoop some rice into the centre of the nori, and make a little well in the centre of the rice. Spoon a quarter of the okaka into this well, then scoop more rice on top. Bring the ends of the nori sheet up over the top of the rice, then bundle the whole thing up in the cling film, and use your hands to shape it into a rounded triangle, compressing firmly as you go. Repeat this process to make four onigiri.

You can eat these warm while they're still fresh, but I think they're better if they sit around for a while, so the nori fully softens and the flavour of the okaka infuses into the rice. Keep them in their cling film, in the refrigerator, then reheat in a steamer or the microwave.

HAM, CUCUMBER AND HORSERADISH SANDWICH

YAMAWASABI HAMU KYŪRI SANDO 山わさびハムきゅうりサンド

MAKES 2 SANDWICHES

¼ cucumber or 1 baby cucumber (thinner,
   Japanese-style cucumbers work best for this)
2 tbsp mayo (ideally Japanese)
2 tbsp horseradish cream
4 slices of white bread
4–6 wafer-thin slices of ham
salt, as needed

METHOD

Slice the cucumbers into thin rounds, then toss with a few pinches of salt. Leave to sit for 20–30 minutes, then squeeze them to expel excess water and pat them dry with paper towel. Stir together the mayo and horseradish, then spread this evenly onto each slice of bread. Arrange the cucumbers and ham on top, then close the sandwiches, cut off their crusts, and cut into triangles. These can be enjoyed right away, or within a day, wrapped in cling film (plastic wrap) and kept in the refrigerator.

ZANGI
(HOKKAIDO-STYLE CHICKEN KARAAGE)

ZANGI ザンギ

The name *zangi* is derived from the Chinese *zhàjī* (fried chicken), and originally appeared on the menu at Torimatsu in Kushiro in 1960. Though a lot of zangi today is basically indistinguishable from standard Japanese karaage, Torimatsu established some unique characteristics of zangi that set it apart: it's cooked on the bone, it uses the whole chicken (instead of just thighs or legs), and it's seasoned with both a marinade and a dipping sauce (called *zantare*). The master at Torimatsu told me they use only wheat flour for frying, but the master at nearby Toriyoshi said they use only potato starch – therefore, I use both. Neither of them would tell me what's in the dipping sauce, so this is just my best approximation!

SERVES 2

'ZANTARE' DIPPING SAUCE
2 tbsp shōyu or tamari
1 tbsp dark brown sugar
1 tbsp tonkatsu sauce
1 tbsp Worcestershire sauce
1 tbsp lemon juice
many shakes of finely ground white pepper

CHICKEN
½ small chicken
6 tbsp sake
4 tbsp shōyu
¼ tsp salt
¼ tsp MSG
1 egg yolk
60 g (2 oz) fresh ginger root, peeled and finely chopped
a few pinches of finely ground white pepper
100 g (3½ oz/⅔ cup) potato starch
100 g (3½ oz/generous ¾ cup) plain (all-purpose) flour
vegetable oil, for deep frying
   (about 2 litres/68 fl oz/8½ cups)
¼ lemon, cut into wedges, to serve (optional)

METHOD
For the zantare, stir everything together until the sugar dissolves.

Cut the chicken into major joints: breast, thigh, drumstick and wing. Using a sharp, heavy knife, cut the thigh into two pieces, through the bone, and cut the breast into four pieces, also through the bone. Cut the wing into two joints.

Combine everything else except the flours and vegetable oil in a large bowl and mix well. Massage the marinade into the chicken. The chicken can be cooked straight away, but I think it is better if it is marinated in the refrigerator for an hour or two (or one day maximum).

Combine the flours in a large bowl. Heat the oil in a deep, wide pan to 170ºC (340°F). Dredge the marinated chicken in the flour, then lower each piece of chicken carefully into the oil, and cook for about 7–8 minutes until golden brown. Use a probe thermometer to check if it's cooked through (the internal temperature should be above 70ºC/158°F) or, failing that, cut into a piece at its thickest point to make sure it's not raw.

Remove the chicken from the oil with chopsticks or tongs and drain on paper towel. Serve with the zantare, and/or the lemon wedges.

SMOKED VENISON SAUSAGE

SHIKANIKU NO KUNSEI SÔSÊJI 鹿肉の燻製ソーセージ

Game and specialty sausage are two things I associate strongly with Hokkaido, found in the refrigerators and freezers of *michi no eki*, local supermarkets, and beer hall and izakaya menus across the island. It makes sense; Hokkaido is a meaty prefecture generally, and the proliferation of Ezo deer makes them common sausage fodder. You will need a meat grinder for this, plus a barbecue or smoker capable of indirect heating. The herbs and spices can be changed to your taste, so feel free to improvise.

MAKES 12 QUITE BIG SAUSAGES OR 16 SAUSAGES OF AVERAGE SIZE

1.2 kg (2 lb 11 oz) lean venison, diced
500 g (1 lb 2 oz) pork fat, diced
10 g (⅓ oz) rice flour
25 g (1 oz) salt
2½ tsp MSG
2½ tsp mustard seeds
½ tsp black pepper
½ tsp dried thyme
½ tsp white pepper
½ tsp dried rosemary
¼ tsp ground ginger
¼ tsp dried sage
¼ tsp paprika
1 garlic clove, grated
40 g (1½ oz) ice water
100 g (3½ oz) rice malt syrup
about 3 metres (10 feet) hog casings, prepared
    according to the manufacturer's instructions

METHOD

Combine the venison, pork fat, rice flour and all of the seasonings in a large bowl and mix well. Run the mixture through a grinder with a coarse plate (8 or 10 mm/⅓ in), then mix in the ice water and malt syrup. Attach a wide nozzle onto your sausage maker and thread the casings onto it, then fill the sausages and tie them into links, however long you like.

Heat some coals in your barbecue or smoker and set it up for indirect cooking. Let the barbecue come up to 110–120°C (230–250°F) and place the sausages on a rack, away from the heat source. Add wood to the coals and cook for about 2 hours, until their internal temperature reaches 75–80°C (167–176°F). Replenish the wood as needed to sustain the smoke.

Once smoked, the sausages will last for about a week in the refrigerator. They can be eaten cold, or grilled (broiled) to crisp their skins.

BIG DISHES &

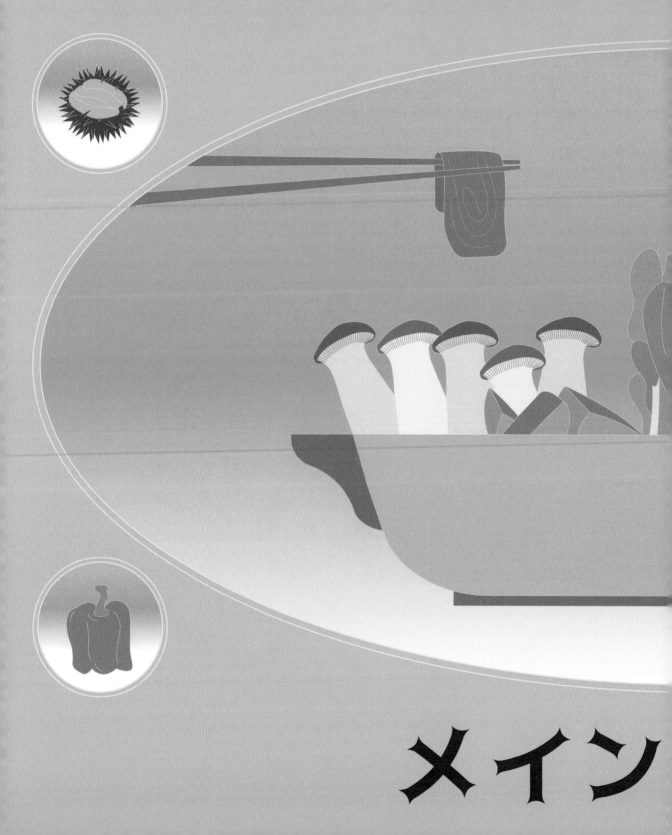

メイン

MAIN MEALS

ディッシュ

明治時代の味

GOTŌKEN: THE MEIJI SET

Hakodate's Gotōken is one of Japan's oldest purveyors of Western food, established in 1879. Though it originally began as a bakery and Russian food restaurant, in 1901 chef Tokujirō Wakayama went to train at the Imperial Hotel in Tokyo. There, he learned to make British curry; this would become the company's signature dish, and one of Hokkaido's most popular omiyage, sold in pouches and tins.[36]

Gotōken has been through a lot over the years. Their premises have burnt down, in 1944 the company was briefly shut by the Hakodate police for serving Western food, and it was requisitioned by Allied GHQ during Japan's postwar occupation. But the company and the curry has endured, maintaining a consistency in their product that now offers customers a taste of history. The restaurant's 'Meiji Set' is a throwback feast showcasing old-school yōshoku cookery at its finest. In addition to the curry and rice, it comes with a variety of side dishes, including crab croquettes, soup and a little cake. It would be pretty hard to recreate the full Meiji Set at home, but I have included recipes for corn potage – because it's very Hokkaido – and for garam masala oil, a clever condiment served alongside the curry.

HAKODATE PORK CURRY

GOTŌKEN FŪ HAKODATE PŌKU KARĒ 五島軒風函館ポークカレー

SERVES 4

30 g (1 oz) butter
20 g (¾ oz) beef dripping
1 onion, finely chopped
2 cm (¾ in) piece fresh ginger root, peeled
   and finely chopped
1 garlic clove, peeled and finely chopped
¼ banana, diced
¼ apple, peeled and grated
2 tbsp Japanese or Madras curry powder
   (hot or mild or a mix of both)
½ tbsp garam masala
1 tbsp turmeric
5 tbsp mango chutney
2 tbsp tomato purée (paste)
50 g (1¾ oz/scant ½ cup) plain (all-purpose) flour
1 tbsp oil
300 g (10½ oz) pork belly, rind off, cut into small pieces
   (a little smaller than bite-size)
1 litre (34 fl oz/4¼ cups) beef stock, or 1 litre
   (34 fl oz/4¼ cups) water plus 2 beef stock cubes
300 g (10½ oz) potatoes, peeled and diced
1 carrot, peeled and diced
¼–½ tsp salt (to taste)
1–2 tbsp shōyu (optional, to taste)

METHOD

Melt the butter and dripping together in a saucepan over a medium heat and add the onion. Cook for about 15 minutes, stirring often, until well browned, then lower the heat and add the ginger, garlic, banana and apple, and cook for a few minutes until the apple softens. Add the spices, chutney and tomato purée and cook for another minute, stirring often, to infuse the spices into the fat, then stir in the flour and cook for a few minutes to form a thick roux. Transfer the roux to a food processor and blend until smooth.

Pour the oil into a casserole and set over a high heat, then add the pork belly and brown for a few minutes on all sides. Add the stock and bring to the boil, then sustain at a low boil for about 45 minutes, until the pork is soft. Add the potatoes and carrots and cook for another 8–10 minutes until tender, then remove all of the meat and vegetables with a slotted spoon and set aside. Tip the roux into the simmering stock, whisking well to break up any clumps (use a stick blender if you want it really smooth), then simmer for a few minutes to thicken. If the sauce is too thick, add a little more water – it should be a pourable consistency. Return the meat and vegetables to the sauce, then season with salt and soy sauce to your taste.

VARIATIONS:

Venison is also a popular choice in Hokkaido curries. Simply follow the recipe as written above, with venison instead of pork, but cook the meat for 1 hour 20 minutes before adding the vegetables. Other protein options include hokki curry, which uses clams (cook them in the stock, then pick out their meat and stir it through at the end) or omu curry, which simply has a soft-set omelette on top.

CORN POTAGE

KÔN POTÂJU コーンポタージュ

MAKES 4-6 SERVINGS
20 g (¾ oz) butter
½ onion, finely diced
150 ml (5 fl oz/scant ⅔ cup) milk
250 ml (8 fl oz fl oz/1 cup) water
1 chicken stock cube
1 tbsp double (heavy) cream
300 g (10½ oz) corn kernels
2 tbsp white wine
salt and white pepper, to taste
a few sprigs of parsley, finely chopped
a handful of croutons

METHOD
Melt the butter in a saucepan over a medium heat
and add the onion. Cook for about 10 minutes, stirring
frequently, until softened, then add the milk, water,
stock cube, double cream and all of the corn except
3–4 spoonfuls. Bring to a boil and cook for about
5 minutes, then add the wine, salt and pepper and cook
for another 5 minutes. Use a blender to purée the soup
until very smooth, then pass through a sieve and return
to the pan along with the remaining corn kernels. Bring
back to a simmer, taste and adjust seasoning as you like.
To serve, ladle into little soup cups and garnish with
a tiny bit of parsley and a few croutons.

GARAM MASALA OIL

GARAMU MASARA OIRU ガラムマサラオイル

MAKES ABOUT 100 ML (3½ FL OZ/SCANT ½ CUP)
5 tbsp oil
3 tbsp garam masala

METHOD
Combine the oil and the garam masala in a saucepan,
stir well and set over a low heat. Heat until the spices
just begin to sizzle, then immediately remove from heat
and leave to infuse as it cools. Keep in a jar and stir
well before using.

イ

カ

の

街

HAKODATE

函館

EXO-KUN

MASCOT: EXO-KUN

Exo-kun, who has a hat in the shape of a squid bearing the image of the night view from Mt Hakodate, bangs representing the waves of the Tsugaru Strait, and clothes representing Hakodate's famous red brick warehouses emblazoned with a sakura-filled outline of Goryōkaku.

© 2016 HAKODATEKAI

ETYMOLOGY

Thought to be from the Ainu *hak casi*, meaning 'shallow fort'. The kanji transliteration means 'box building'. Both may refer to a castle built by the Kōno Clan in the 15th century.

POPULATION: 241,747

函館

HAKODATE

函館

Hakodate is mostly known for two things: ramen, and the night view of the city from the summit of Mt Hakodate. The view is considered one of the finest in Japan. If you run a Google image search for Hakodate, you will be presented with a collage of glittering night view shots, the city and its suburbs framed by the black sea on either side of the Kameda Peninsula, a toe-like protrusion of the larger Oshima Peninsula – which is more like an isthmus than a peninsula. But I did not come to Hakodate to discuss the differences between isthmuses and peninsulae. I came to eat.

But also, I came to Hakodate because if you're going to Hokkaido, Hakodate is a logical starting point. It's one of those cities, like Asahikawa, that feels like a trading post of a town that seems to exist mostly to connect people and things to other places.

From the early 1700s it was dominated by the Matsumae clan and the Tokugawa shogunate, who jointly fortified the peninsula to control trade between Japan, Ezo and the Kuril Islands. Hakodate was already a busy port by the time Commodore Perry arrived in 1854, and was one of the first sites in Japan that opened to international trade prior to the Meiji Restoration.

Ever since, Hakodate has been a place of coming and going. It's the terminus of the shinkansen, it has the second largest airport in Hokkaido, and is a port of call along several ferry routes. As a major junction for trade and travel, Hakodate's food culture is more connected to commerce and industry than it is to the natural environment. Yes, there is kaisendon, though this is better in other parts of Hokkaido rather than at Hakodate's famous Morning Market. But you can have a go at catching your own squid there! So that's fun.

Since so much Hokkaido produce ends up funnelling through Hakodate, it draws in local specialities from other cities, as well. You can easily find ikameshi (Mori), pork yakitori (Muroran) and uni (Rishiri) in Hakodate. But you can also find highly idiosyncratic local foods, too – none more zany than the offerings at Lucky Pierrot.

Lucky Pierrot is a fast food chain with a broad, crowd-pleasing menu of B-grade gourmet favourites, and over-the-top, sometimes surreal interior decorating. One branch, for example, has a year-round Christmas theme, with miniature Santas everywhere. Lucky Pierrot was founded by Ichirō Oh, the son of Chinese immigrants from Kobe, who wanted his restaurants to capture the excitement of the circus he felt when he was a boy. In keeping with this mission, Lucky Pierrot's logo and mascot is a colourful clown, with a vaguely menacing look in his black, starry eyes.

函館

HAKODATE

函館

→

Although Lucky Pierrot is absolutely ridiculous, they take their food and their Hakodate identity seriously; they source as much as they can from southern Hokkaido, and have turned down opportunities to open branches outside of Hakodate. Lucky Pierrot's most famous dish is its 'Chinese chicken', but it is also known for the Futoccho ('fatso') burger, a behemoth with more than a dozen layers. For me, this is far more of a draw to Hakodate than the night view, far more spectacular and stunning. I've seen enough big cities by now to rarely feel dazzled by their bright lights.

But a burger which stands a solid 10 inches tall? Now that is a thing of beauty.

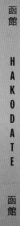

チャイニーズチキン

THE FATSO BURGER
HOMAGE TO LUCKY PIERROT

LUCKY PIERROT NO 'FUTOCCHO BÃGÃ' NO OMÃJU ラッキーピエローの「フトッチョバーガー」のオマージュ

The Futoccho Burger is more delicious than anything so absurd has any right to be. Like Lucky Pierrot itself, it seems more designed to provoke a 'wtf' sort of reaction than to be good. But then you taste it – and damn, it's delicious. It is not difficult to cook but it requires careful coordination in terms of *mise en place* and cook times. Read and understand the method, and make sure you have everything ready before dropping the burgers in the pan.

PER BURGER - LISTED IN THE ORDER YOU STACK THEM, BOTTOM TO TOP:

sesame seed bun (bottom)
mayo, about 1 tbsp
125 g (4½ oz) beef patty, seasoned with a generous
    amount of salt on both sides
1 slice of American cheese
diced white onion
about 2 tbsp Meat Sauce (page 242)
1 large Meat and Potato Croquette (page 91)
tonkatsu sauce, about 2 tbsp
1 fried egg
another 125 g (4½ oz) beef patty, seasoned
1 more slice of American cheese
more white onion
another 2 tbsp Meat Sauce
1 thick slice of tomato
vast amounts of iceberg lettuce
more mayo
sesame seed bun (top)

METHOD

You will also need oil, for shallow and deep frying, and a long skewer or thin chopstick, to keep this all together. Start with the croquette. Fry it first (as per the instructions on page 91), then keep it hot on a wire rack in an oven set to 100°C fan (225°F). Have the bottom and top buns ready, warm and spread with mayo. The meat sauce should be in a small, microwave-safe container. All of the other garnishes should be prepped and laid out.

Heat about a teaspoon of oil in a large, non-stick or cast-iron frying pan or griddle over a high heat until smoking. Lay the beef patties into the pan, smashing them with a spatula so they flatten. Cook for about 3 minutes, to form a crust, then flip them over and top each one with a slice of cheese and some diced onion. Crack the egg into the pan, then re-heat the meat sauce for about 30 seconds in the microwave. At this point, the burgers should have been cooking on the other side for another 3 minutes and will be just about done. Flip over the egg, and switch off the heat.

Assemble the burgers as written above. Stick the skewer into the completed burger to keep it together. Foolhardy rogues may attempt to eat this with their hands; dainty pragmatists may opt for a knife and fork. Either way, this will require many napkins.

SAPPORO

札
幌

TEREBI TŌSAN

MASCOT: TEREBI TŌSAN
Several, representing various wards, landmarks and municipal campaigns. My favourite is Terebi Tōsan ('TV Dad') who represents the Sapporo TV Tower.

POPULATION: 1,959,750

ETYMOLOGY
From the Ainu *sat poro pet*, 'dry, great river' believed to be a reference to what is now called the Toyohira River.

Munich, Pilsen, Milwaukee, Sapporo: some cities are simply synonymous with suds. Of course, Sapporo is known for many things: the Snow Festival, miso ramen and the Hokkaido Shrine, to name a few. But still, if anybody knows anything about Sapporo, that thing is bound to be Sapporo Beer.

Sapporo Brewery is the oldest brewery in Japan, originally founded in 1876, one of several established by the government to rapidly develop Hokkaido, which is particularly amenable to growing barley and hops.

In 1903, Sapporo Brewery acquired a sugar factory northeast of Sapporo's city centre. It still stands today, in all its red-brick, neo-colonial, Meiji-era glory, as part of a complex known as the Sapporo Beer Garden. It houses a museum and various venues in which to knock back fabulously fresh Sapporo beer, accompanied by world-class drinking food. The most impressive of these venues is the great Kessel Hall, with its all-you-can-drink beer, all-you-can-eat Genghis Khan (page 131), and towering copper kettle, which looms over the space like a monument. Kessel Hall is one of Japan's great venues for socialising. The room itself is a conversation starter, historic and grand, and of course, the whole place is just silly with alcohol.

I first visited the Sapporo Beer Garden when I was 20, barely old enough to legally drink. It was all so exciting, but then again, isn't everything when you're 20? I entered that great hall and I was properly awed by it, and I wore a big bib and ate Genghis Khan and drank mug after mug of Sapporo beer until I could eat and drink no more. I stumbled out into the world, which had turned a light golden hue as if seen through a beer glass. As I watched the sun set from the window of the bus, I gleefully thought to myself, '*I'm drunk in a foreign country!*' – surely one of the dumbest, purest thoughts I have ever had, but I was so smashed, so full of grilled lamb, so free and so happy to be alive.

Almost 20 years later, I finally returned to Kessel Hall – and I am pleased to report that it remains as impressive as ever. The towering copper kettle still draws the eye, upwards from the bustling bar below. The air is thick with a visible smog of vapourised lamb fat; when you sit down at your table the hostess hands you a big plastic bag to put your outerwear in, so it doesn't end up reeking of meat. The beer is just as cold and crisp as I remember it; the lamb, just as tender.

But this time, the effects of so much alcohol and red meat hit a lot harder. My decrepit middle-aged body can't handle it. Instead of feeling warm and fuzzy at the end of the bacchanal, I left Kessel Hall feeling bloated, sweaty and uncomfortable. I got on the bus and watched the lights of the city blur by and once again thought 'I'm drunk in a foreign country', but this time, with a feeling of abject remorse, not revelry. There's something endearing about a wide-eyed 20-year-old rube putting on a bib and getting blotto by himself in a beer

→

hall. But there's something sad and weird about a jaded 38-year-old with a dad bod and a bald spot doing the same thing.

Lesson learned: you can't go back to Kessel Hall again. Nostalgia and all-you-can-drink beer are a dangerous mix. Of course, that's not to say you can't enjoy Genghis Khan at any age – of course you can. But you can only enjoy it for the first time once.

GENGHIS KHAN
(GRILLED LAMB AND VEGETABLES)

JINGISUKAN ジンギスカン

There are several theories as to how this dish of grilled lamb and vegetables came to be, but they all generally involve fanciful visions of Mongolian sheep-based feasting combined with real northeastern Chinese cuisine, which became more familiar to the Japanese following the invasion of Manchuria in 1931. This coincided with an increase in sheep farming in Hokkaido, initially for wool production.

The dish has little to do with Mongolia. But you do get to feel like a real barbarian when you eat it. You sit down and are brought a large stein of cold lager, trayfuls of lamb and vegetables, and that most noble piece of military armour: a disposable bib. You cook everything on a dome-shaped cast iron griddle, meant to evoke Mongolian shields. As soon as the food is cooked to your liking, you snatch it from the hot plate with chopsticks and dip it in a tangy sauce, then shovel it into your mouth, in between glugs of beer.

The late Jonathan Gold once said that 'taco' ought to be a verb, a fluid movement from the griddle to your mouth. As is Genghis Khan: sizzle, dip, chomp, swallow, swig.

SERVES 4

700–800 g (1 lb 9–1 lb 12 oz) lamb shoulder or loin, boneless and trimmed of excess fat

FOR THE TARE

120 ml (4 fl oz/½ cup) shōyu
4 tbsp beer
½ apple, peeled and cored
¼ small onion
1 small garlic clove
1.5 cm (½ in) fresh ginger root, peeled and thinly sliced
3 tbsp mirin
3 tbsp honey
2 tbsp light brown sugar
1 tbsp vinegar
juice of ½ lemon
1 tbsp sesame seeds
¼ tsp pepper
pinch chilli powder

1–2 tbsp lamb fat, butter or vegetable oil
¼ small kabocha, butternut squash or similar, cut into slices about 2 cm (¾ in) thick
½ pointed cabbage, cut into strips about 2 cm (¾ in) wide
1 onion, halved and cut into half-rounds about 5 mm (¼ in) thick
100 g (3½ oz) bean sprouts

METHOD

Place the lamb in the freezer for about 30 minutes to firm it up. Meanwhile, combine all of the tare ingredients in a blender and purée. Then cut the lamb into very thin slices against the grain.

Set up a camping stove or induction hob on the table and bring over all the raw ingredients for people to cook themselves. Divide the tare into little individual dipping bowls for each person. Place a wide skillet or griddle on the burner and set over a high heat. Melt the lamb fat, butter or oil in the pan, then cook the lamb and vegetables to your liking, dip them into the tare, and enjoy. You can also do this on a barbecue, but you will need a very fine mesh grille or perforated metal plate to go over the coals.

If communal cooking is not practical, simply heat the largest pan or griddle you have over a high heat, add the fat and then cook the lamb and vegetables all together until nicely browned – it should take about 10 minutes. Bring to the table and serve with the tare on the side.

SHIKABE

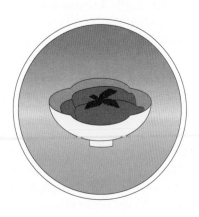

鹿部

鹿部

S H I K A B E

鹿部

鹿部

S H I K A B E

鹿部

Shikabe lies along the entrance to Uchiura Bay on a little bump of land created by the eruption of Mt Komagatake many centuries ago. On the road from Hakodate to Shikabe, there's evidence of this seismic activity everywhere. The sharply defined caldera of Mt Komagatake looms, omnipresent, in the distance. In Shikabe itself, geothermal vents where people can use the natural steam to cook food and, most strikingly, a geyser, which has been roped off and put on display behind the town's visitor centre, like a wild animal in a zoo. It is truly weird to see, like the earth itself has sprung a leak.

Uchiura Bay is apparently nicknamed 'Eruption Bay', because it is flanked by three active volcanoes, with a few more just a lava-launched stone's throw away. The flow of magma into the gulf has enriched the water with vital minerals that have made it teem with life, which traditionally sustained Ainu villages, and are now important commercial products. One of these products is kombu of excellent quality, a genuine source of local pride.

Later, I learn why, on a visit a local kombu farmer. His name is Īda-san, and his family has been fishing in Shikabe for 300 years, but began kombu farming about 40 years ago. His small operation – just him and his son – produce tonnes of the green stuff each year, all harvested, sun-dried and packaged by hand. I am taken up in a chain-pulleyed lift to the warehouse above their workshop, where I enter what can only be described as an enormous blue plastic bag, piled high with gauze-bound bales of kombu. The room's cobalt glow and permeating smell of the sea gave it a dream-like quality. I felt like a merman.

As I stood in the warehouse, dwarfed by Īda-san's bounty, I felt a renewed sense of kombu's importance at the core of Japanese cookery. I will always be an instant dashi advocate – it's delicious, cheap and makes cooking Japanese food so simple and convenient. But it is, ultimately, just a simulacrum – a shadow on the wall of Plato's kombu cave.

As we left, Īda-san graciously handed me two types of his kombu to take home. I intended to make the most of them, but I wound up giving them away as gifts. I guess, in a way, that is making the most of them.

GRIDDLED SALMON AND VEGETABLES WITH MISO AND MELTED BUTTER

CHANCHAN-YAKI ちゃんちゃん焼き

I learned to cook this Hokkaido comfort food classic from Toshi-chan in Shikabe, a fisherman's wife who organises cooking classes at the town hall. The inclusion of mayonnaise is Toshi-chan's own twist. It is not typical, but I think it's delicious, so I've included it, too. I also learned to make it with just cabbage and onions, though other vegetables are common, as well – carrots and shimeji mushrooms in particular appear in a lot of recipes, so feel free to add them if you like.

SERVES 4

80 g (2¾ oz) miso (white is best but red is fine, too)
4 tbsp sake
2 tbsp mirin
1 tbsp caster (superfine) sugar
1 tbsp mayo
2 tbsp butter
½ sweetheart (hispi) cabbage, cut into strips about 2 cm (¾ in) wide
2 onions, halved and thinly sliced
about 500 g (1 lb 2 oz) salmon, boneless (you can have the skin on or off, but if you leave it on, it needs to be scaled)

METHOD

Combine the miso, sake, mirin, sugar and mayo in a small bowl, stirring with a fork or small whisk until no lumps remain. Add 1 tbsp of the butter to a very wide, non-stick or well-seasoned cast iron pan or griddle over a medium–high heat, then add all of the vegetables and stir-fry for 1–2 minutes, just to coat in the butter and barely start to cook. Push the vegetables off to the side of the pan, and place the salmon in the middle, skin-side up. Leave to cook for 2–3 minutes, then turn the fish over so it is skin-side down, being careful not to break the flesh. Pour the miso sauce all over the fish and vegetables, lower the heat to medium, and cover the pan with a lid or a sheet of kitchen foil. Leave everything to steam-fry for about 10–12 minutes, until the salmon is cooked through. Once the fish is done, place the remaining 1 tbsp of butter on top of the salmon and let it melt. Bring the whole pan to the table to serve, along with rice, soup and pickles.

OVERNIGHT-DRIED FISH

SAKANA NO ICHIYA-BOSHI NO TSUKURIKATA 魚の一夜干しの作り方

The seas surrounding Hokkaido are home to what may be my favourite fish: hokke. Their flavour is like a cross between herring and and cod, with distinct scallop-like notes. It is almost impossible for me to go to an izakaya in Hokkaido and not order hokke. I am a hokke-holic.

The fish itself is only part of what makes it so delicious. How it is prepared and cooked is important, too. Hokke, like many other fish in Hokkaido, is often dried overnight (*ichiya boshi*), which is actually a two-day process, as the fish is brined first. The results are exquisite. The brine seasons and firms the flesh, and allows it to retain moisture during oooking, while the drying concentrates its flavour and creates a wonderfully crisp skin.

You can use any oily fish for this – this recipe uses mackerel as it is widely available and delicious, you can use the same process to make *shiozake* (salt-cured salmon), but increase the amount of salt to 50 g (1¾ oz).

SERVES 2-4

600 ml (20 fl oz/2½ cups) water
4 tbsp sake
30 g (1 oz) salt
2 whole, very fresh mackerel, cleaned, butterflied and skin scored
grated daikon or radish, as needed
ponzu, as needed

METHOD

Stir together the water, sake and salt until the salt dissolves, then pour this over the mackerel. Cover and place in the refrigerator overnight. The next day, remove the mackerel from the brine and pat them dry, then place on a wire rack, uncovered, in the refrigerator overnight again.

When the surface of the fish is totally dry to the touch, it is ready to cook (but it can also be kept in the refrigerator, covered, for another few days). To cook, simply grill (ideally over charcoal) on both sides for a few minutes until cooked through. Enjoy with grated daikon or radish and a bit of ponzu.

ASHIBETSU

芦別

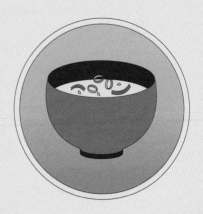

ASHIBŌ

芦別 ASHIBETSU 芦別

芦別 ASHIBETSU 芦別

Look towards the mountains from Ashibetsu Station and you'll notice the 88 metre tall Great Kannon of Hokkaido. The statue was constructed in 1989, as part of the Kita no Miyako 'leisure land', established in 1968 as a multi-facility attraction intended to drive a new economy based on tourism, amidst the rapid closure of Ashibetsu's many coal mines. Another theme park, 'Canadian World' – inspired by the fictional town of Avonlea from *Anne of Green Gables* – opened in 1990.

For a while, tourism was steady, but it never came close to the city's projections. People bypassed Ashibetsu in favour of Furano and Biei's irresistible flower fields or the ramen shops and bars of Asahikawa. Municipal investment in Canadian World created such a scandalous amount of public debt that it prompted Ashibetsu's mayor to resign in 1995. It was shut and converted to a public park in 1999.[38] Kita no Miyako followed suit, going into liquidation in 2008. As for the Great Kannon, it was acquired by a private Buddhist organisation in 2013 and is no longer open to the public. But the bodhisattva of mercy and compassion, 'she who hears the cries of the world', still stands, solemnly watching over Ashibetsu.

Ashibetsu's population peaked at 70,000 in the mid-20th century; it is now less than a sixth of that. Ashibetsu's population peaked at 70,000 in the mid-20th century; it is now less than a sixth of that. There are signs of life: cars passing through, people getting off trains and onto buses, schoolkids carrying band instruments. But this doesn't stop Ashibetsu from feeling like a ghost town: pachinko parlours overgrown with moss, rusted-out rooftops, and damp-stained menus in the windows of shuttered restaurants, never to be ordered from again. Sun-bleached stickers bearing Ashibetsu's slogan memorialise more optimistic times: 'the home of shooting stars'.

I was in Ashibetsu for one thing: *gatatan*. After wandering around the city, I settled on one of several restaurants that specialise in it: Hōka Hanten. Like the rest of the town, at first it looked dead. The lights were off, and there was no one inside except the owner, sitting in the far corner of the kitchen, reading a newspaper. It wasn't clear that it was actually open.

But as soon as I entered, the place began to feel warm and inviting. The owner put down her newspaper and greeted me with a smile. We chatted a bit. I looked at the hand-written menu on the wall. She asked if I could read it. I said mostly, but it didn't matter anyway – I knew what I wanted. Gatatan. No noodles. And some gyoza.

Her husband entered. He was just as warm and welcoming. The gyoza arrived. He told me they were handmade, even the wrappers. They were outstanding – I couldn't remember having such good gyoza in recent or even distant memory. They had picked up the flavour of what was clearly a well-seasoned cast iron pan. Their skins were supple and plumply stuffed with a loose but not crumbly filling, flavoured with handfuls of negi, nira, garlic and ginger. They were perfect.

→

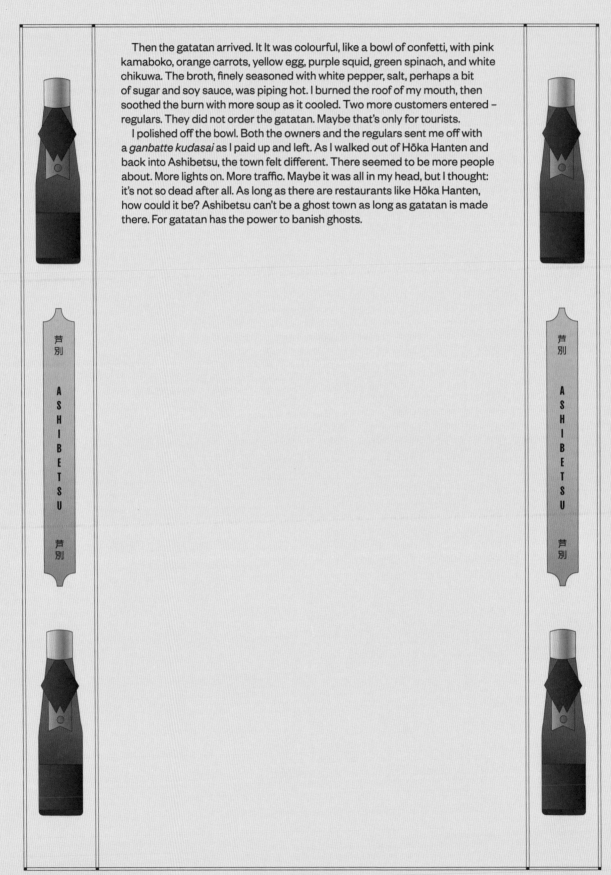

Then the gatatan arrived. It It was colourful, like a bowl of confetti, with pink kamaboko, orange carrots, yellow egg, purple squid, green spinach, and white chikuwa. The broth, finely seasoned with white pepper, salt, perhaps a bit of sugar and soy sauce, was piping hot. I burned the roof of my mouth, then soothed the burn with more soup as it cooled. Two more customers entered – regulars. They did not order the gatatan. Maybe that's only for tourists.

I polished off the bowl. Both the owners and the regulars sent me off with a *ganbatte kudasai* as I paid up and left. As I walked out of Hōka Hanten and back into Ashibetsu, the town felt different. There seemed to be more people about. More lights on. More traffic. Maybe it was all in my head, but I thought: it's not so dead after all. As long as there are restaurants like Hōka Hanten, how could it be? Ashibetsu can't be a ghost town as long as gatatan is made there. For gatatan has the power to banish ghosts.

芦別 ASHIBETSU 芦別

芦別 ASHIBETSU 芦別

星 の 降 る 里

GATATAN
(THICK CHINESE-STYLE MINERS' SOUP)

GATATAN ガタタン

Gatatan is a thick, Chinese-style soup, containing a multitude of ingredients, including meat, seafood and vegetables. It is filling and nutritious but also cheap, a perfect meal for the miners that once made up the majority of Ashibetsu's workforce. Although the mines have long since shut, the people of Ashibetsu have made a concerted effort to preserve and promote gatatan as a matter of local pride.[39]

It is originally based on a Manchurian dish called *gēda tāng*, named for little flour dumplings called *gēda*. The soup was introduced to Ashibetsu in the 1950s by Bungonosuke Murai, who learned to make the dish while living in China during Japanese occupation. The fortifying nature of gatatan made it a hit not only with miners, but also with drunks.[40] But you don't have to be a drunken miner to enjoy it. You just need to be in the mood for a hot, nutritious, soupy hug.

SERVES 4

DUMPLINGS
60 g (2 oz/½ cup) plain (all-purpose) flour
15 g (½ oz) rice flour (non-glutinous)
30 ml (2 tbsp) just-boiled water

SOUP
1 tbsp oil
120 g (4¼ oz) pork (any cut)
¼ onion
4 leaves Chinese leaf (napa cabbage)
4 leaves sweetheart (hispi) or flat cabbage
½ carrot, peeled
60–70 g (2–2½ oz) baby squid
2 tbsp sake
1.4 litres (47⅓ fl oz/6 cups) water,
   or light pork broth (unseasoned)
40 g (1½ oz) kamaboko
40 g (1½ oz) chikuwa
50 g (1¾ oz) bamboo shoots
5 g (¼ oz) *kikurage*, rehydrated
1 tbsp chicken powder
1 tbsp shōyu
½ tsp sesame oil
¼ tsp salt, or more to taste
white pepper, to taste (use a generous amount)
4 eggs, beaten
6 tbsp potato starch, mixed with
   100 ml (3½ fl oz/scant ½ cup) water
a handful of spinach (large leaf),
   washed and coarsely chopped

METHOD
Make the dumpling dough by kneading together the flours and water until they form a soft but dry dough. Knead only enough to bring the dough together so you don't develop the gluten too much. Shape the dough into a log about an inch thick. Wrap in cling film (plastic wrap) and rest in the refrigerator for at least an hour.

All of the ingredients should be cut into small, thin pieces; they should be small enough so that you can get several different things in one spoonful, but not so small that they have no texture. Heat the oil in a saucepan, then add the pork and onion and sauté for about 5 minutes, until the onion has softened. Add the cabbages, carrot and squid, and sauté for another couple of minutes.

Add the sake, water or broth, fish cakes, bamboo shoots, kikurage and all of the seasonings and bring to a low boil.

Unwrap the dumpling dough and cut it into coin-shaped slices, then drop them into the soup. Stir, then bring the soup back to the boil and cook for 5 minutes, stirring occasionally.

Pour the beaten egg into the soup while stirring slowly, so it forms thick strands within the soup. Reduce the heat to a low simmer and drizzle in the potato starch slurry. Simmer for a few minutes to thicken, then stir in the spinach. Adjust seasoning as you like, then serve piping hot, in large, deep bowls.

SALMON, TOFU AND VEGETABLE HOTPOT

ISHIKARI NABE 石狩鍋

Ishikari nabe, from its namesake town of Ishikari (page 77), is a very satisfying salmon and tofu hotpot. This recipe is modelled after the 'original' version served at Kindaitei but modern versions contain many more ingredients including potatoes, daikon, mushrooms, corn and butter. Though not typical, I also like to season this with a small dash of ponzu. This recipe also calls for the meaty trim from a filleted salmon so either ask a fishmonger for this or buy a whole salmon, make any number of delicious Hokkaido salmon dishes (see the diagram on pages 148–149 as a guide), and save the trim yourself.

SERVES 4

15 g (½ oz) kombu
300 g (10½ oz) salmon ara (meaty salmon trim, spine bones, heads, etc.)
1 litre (34 fl oz/4¼ cups) water
4 tbsp sake
2 small onions, sliced about 1 cm (½ in) thick
4 fresh shiitake mushrooms, destemmed and halved
1 tbsp usukuchi shōyu
1 tsp caster (superfine) sugar
80 g (2¾ oz) white miso
½ sweetheart (hispi) cabbage, coarsely chopped
250 g (9 oz) salmon, deboned, scaled and cut into bite-size chunks
1 block (300 g/10½ oz) firm silken tofu
a handful (about 40 g/1½ oz) of shungiku
chilli (hot pepper) flakes, ponzu and/or sanshō, to taste (optional)

METHOD

Place the kombu in the bottom of a large hotpot or casserole dish and add the ara and water, then leave to soak for 1–2 hours. Set over a low heat, and slowly bring to a low boil. As the liquid boils, carefully skim away the scum that forms on the surface. It will take about 10–15 minutes of boiling before all of the scum stops forming. Once it does, remove the kombu.

Add the sake, onions, shiitake, shōyu, sugar and miso, using a ladle or strainer to hold the miso as you whisk it into the dashi to avoid lumps. Continue to boil for 3–4 minutes, then add the cabbage, salmon and tofu, and cook for another 3–4 minutes until the salmon is just cooked through. Add the shungiku and let it wilt into the broth, then serve immediately. Garnish with chilli and/or sanshō, to taste (it should not be spicy).

THE WHOL

LOIN AND FILLETS

SHIOZAKE (OVERNIGHT-DRIED FISH) (PAGE 138)
ABASHIRI SALMON ZANGI DON (PAGE 176)
CEP OHAW (PAGE 42)
HASAMI-ZUKE (PAGE 54)
ISHIKARI NABE (PAGE 146)
SANPEI-JIRU (PAGE 53)
CHANCHAN YAKI (PAGE 136)
RUIBE (PAGE 32)

HEAD

CITATAP (PAGE 32)
ISHIKARI NABE (PAGE 146)
NOSE CARTILAGE SALAD (PAGE 77)

BELLY

NORI-WRAPPED BELLY (PAGE 78)
KATTE-DON (PAGE 184)

E SALMON

A USER'S GUIDE

OFFAL

IKURA (PAGE 184)
SHIRAKO (PAGE 77)
MEFUN (PAGE 77)
LIVER PÂTÉ (PAGE 77)
GYOSHŌ (PAGE 176)

ARA (TRIM – FINS AND TAIL)

ISHIKARI NABE (PAGE 146)
SANPEI-JIRU (PAGE 53)

HOKKAIDO RAMEN

AN OVERVIEW

Conditions in Hokkaido make for a perfect storm of great ramen. It ticks all the boxes:

- History of trade and itinerant labour from China
- Climatological limitations on rice cultivation
- Unique agriculture and aquaculture that yields many key ramen ingredients
- It's cold as hell – perfect ramen weather

Hokkaido is widely known for three famous varieties of regional ramen: Hakodate shio, Sapporo miso and Asahikawa shōyu. But Hokkaido's ramen culture goes way beyond that. For starters, there are micro-styles, unique bowls served by individual shops throughout the prefecture, such as Asahikawa's Santōka and Morumen (page 163), Isono Kazuo's 'Sapporo Black', and Teshikaga Ramen. Then there are lesser-known regional ramen such as Rishiri kombu Ramen, Kushiro Ramen (page 164) and Muroran Curry Ramen (pages 167–168). It is remarkable to have so many local ramen styles all in one prefecture. What's even more remarkable is that all of these styles are so distinctive.

HOW TO USE THE RECIPES

All ramen is made essentially the same way. You must first have broth, tare, noodles, oil or fat, and toppings ready to go. Each regional ramen recipe here is based on elemental recipes found on pages 229–234, with a few extra additions and techniques explained within the recipe itself.

To make a basic bowl of ramen, have the broth at a simmer, the tare and oil warm, the bowl pre-heated, and the toppings prepped. Boil the noodles only after everything else is ready. They will only take about 30–90 seconds to cook (depending on the noodle), and you don't want the cooked noodles to sit around while you prepare the rest of the dish. While the noodles are cooking, combine the broth, tare and oil in the bowl, then tip the drained noodles into the soup before adding the toppings. (There are some exceptions to this method, which are also explained in each recipe.)

Toppings are provided without specific quantities; all ramen can be garnished to your taste, but as a general rule, less is more. You want to be able to enjoy the noodles and broth on their own, without too much clutter.

SAPPORO MISO RAMEN

SAPPORO MISO RÂMEN 札幌味噌ラーメン

Miso ramen is criminally misunderstood. Here in the UK, anyway, a lot of 'miso ramen' is just ordinary miso soup with noodles plonked into it. I suppose that is, technically, miso ramen. But it's miso ramen in the same sense that instant coffee is coffee: an upsetting, watery betrayal.

Real Sapporo miso ramen is a marriage of full-bodied broth and complex miso tare, fused together in a wok with plenty of hot lard. You need the fat and gelatine of a good meat broth to create something tactile and viscous, coating the noodles like a sauce so every mouthful carries a huge whack of flavour.

But where did it come from? Well, as it turns out, it sort of *was* originally just noodles plonked into miso soup. I defer to Sapporo ramen scholar Mike 'Ramen Lord' Satinover for the history (and for the tare and noodle recipes, which are originally derived from his[40]):

> First wave: in 1956 Aji no Sanpei creates miso ramen, basically by accident. They're making a pork miso soup and a customer asks for them to put noodles in it. So the legend goes … They also establish the noodle style, working with Nishiyama Seimen to develop a curly, dense noodle with egg…

> Second wave, 1964: Sumire is created. They invent the 'lard-cap style' of miso, denoted for a thick layer of melted fat trapping the heat below. Sumire later reopens in 1989 after the brothers who ran it split; one brother creates Sumire as a new shop, the other later opens 'Junren,' a misreading of the original shop's kanji, 純連.[41]

Satinover continues to describe a 'third wave' of Sapporo miso ramen, in which various shops build upon and diverge from the templates created by Aji no Sanpei, Sumire and Junren. All three of these hugely influential shops are still going strong, and you should definitely visit them. (Aji no Sanpei, weirdly, is currently located inside a stationery store.)

Miso ramen is one of the more complicated styles to make. But once you understand the process, it's not that hard. There are a few key things to consider. First, use unpasteurised miso if you can get it; the flavour will be much fuller and more complex. Second, when stir-frying the veg, be sure to cook them quickly and lightly; they will continue to soften in the broth when you add it to the wok, so err on the side of under-cooking.

Finally: the iconic toppings of butter and corn are often dismissed by ramen dorks as 'for tourists' … but like, who cares? I'm not sure that's even true, and more to the point, it's one of the worst reasons imaginable to deprive yourself of such obvious deliciousness.

MISO TARE

MAKES 400 G/14 OZ (ENOUGH FOR ABOUT 7-8 BOWLS)
250 g (9 oz) white miso
25 g (1 oz) dark red miso (such as Hatchō)
25 g (1 oz) moromi miso
2 tbsp lard
½ small onion (50 g/1¾ oz), finely chopped
15 g (½ oz) fresh ginger root, peeled and finely chopped
12 garlic cloves (about 1 bulb), finely chopped
1 tbsp ground coriander
⅓ tsp gochugaru or similar chilli (hot pepper) flakes
⅛ tsp ground white pepper
1 tsp tomato purée (paste)
4 tbsp sake
2 tbsp mirin
1 tbsp Demerara sugar
2 tbsp olive oil
1 tbsp sesame oil

METHOD

Stir together the misos until evenly blended. Heat the lard in a saucepan or small frying pan over a medium heat, and once it melts, add the onion. Sauté for about 10 minutes until browned, then add the ginger and all but two of the garlic cloves. Sauté for another 3–4 minutes until the garlic browns a bit, then add the spices, tomato purée, and about a third of the miso mixture. Fry the paste for about 5 minutes until the miso begins to smell like toffee, then add the sake and mirin and stir well. Let the mixture boil for about 5 minutes to cook off the alcohol, then remove from the heat and stir in the sugar, olive oil and sesame oil. Leave to cool to room temperature, then transfer to a blender or food processor along with the rest of the miso and remaining garlic and purée until smooth. Keep in the refrigerator until ready to use.

PER BOWL

50–60 g (1¾–2 oz) miso tare
1–2 tbsp hot, melted lard
300 ml (10 fl oz/1¼ cups) Dōbutsu-Kei Broth (page 229)
Sapporo-Style Noodles (page 223)
¼ onion, thinly sliced
a handful of flat or pointed cabbage, coarsely chopped
a handful of bean sprouts
a spoonful of minced (ground) pork
spring onions (scallions)

OPTIONAL TOPPINGS

a few slices of carrot, red (bell) pepper, kikurage
    or shiitake, to stir-fry (see method)
butter
corn
thread-cut chilli or chilli (hot pepper) flakes
chāshū, thinly sliced or cut into batons (see method)
menma
wild garlic or wild leeks
ajitama

METHOD

Most Sapporo miso ramen shops incorporate stir-fried vegetables and minced pork, which is briefly boiled in seasoned soup. To do this, add the lard to a wok and place over a very high heat. Once the fat is shimmering, add the onions, cabbage, bean sprouts (and any other veg you might want to add, but don't overdo it) and minced pork, and stir-fry for a couple minutes until lightly charred but still quite crunchy. Add the miso tare to the wok, let it caramelise briefly, then add the broth and stir well. Cook the noodles as the broth comes to the boil; they should take about the same amount of time. Drain the noodles, tip them into the bowl, then pour over the broth and stir-fried vegetables. Garnish with spring onions and serve.

A note about chāshū: some Sapporo miso ramen is served without chāshū at all. Some of it has nice big slices, as you'd find in most ramen. But Junren has chāshū cut into little strips. I quite like these because of how they slurp – they get lost in the broth and tangled up in the noodles, so you get chāshū surprises as you work your way through the bowl.

HAKODATE SHIO RAMEN

HAKODATE SHIO RÂMEN 函館塩ラーメン

Ramen, or ramen-like Chinese noodle soups, have been served in Hakodate since the 1880s, and possibly even earlier than that. Hakodate was among a handful of 'treaty ports', open to trade before Japan officially opened to foreign merchants with the Meiji Restoration. As such, Hakodate was frequented by Chinese visitors from the 1850s onwards, conducting their own trade activities as well as acting as liaisons between European powers and the Japanese.[43] As business with China increased, so did the presence of Chinese food in Hakodate, including the noodle soups that would ultimately become Hakodate shio ramen. Many of the ramen-ya in Hakodate retain their Chinese character to some degree in their names and décor, such as Hōran ('phoenix orchid'), established in 1950.

I have always wanted to have a time machine so I could travel back to the 1880s to taste what ramen was like at the point of its inception. But with Hakodate ramen, I feel like I hardly need to – generally, it remains a simple, unembellished, decidedly old-fashioned affair, which makes it one of the hardest types of ramen to really nail. Because the broth and toppings are so austere, I think of these as a showcase for the noodles themselves. So make good ones (page 233) – cook them perfectly and slurp them heartily.

SHIO TARE

water (or dashi; see method)
salt
MSG
sake (optional)

METHOD

A basic shio tare can be made by combining any quantity of water with 10–15% salt and 3–5% MSG. So, for example, 500 ml (17 fl oz/generous 2 cups) water plus 75 g (2½ oz) salt and 25 g (1 oz) MSG will make a strong, salty tare with no extraneous flavours – perfect if you want to highlight the flavour of the broth itself.

However, you can also add complexity and aroma by using dashi instead of water. Strong fishy flavours are not typical in Hakodate ramen (unless you are making a kaisen ramen; see opposite), so avoid using kezuribushi or niboshi. Instead opt for more subtle aromas like kombu and dried scallops. Once you have made a dashi, then it's just a matter of adding enough salt and MSG to turn it into a concentrated seasoning. I also use a small amount of sake to add subtle notes of sweetness, acidity and fragrance.

DASHI-BASED SHIO TARE

300 ml (10 fl oz/1¼ cups) dried scallop or kombu dashi
    (or better yet, a mix of both – see page 241)
1 tbsp sake
45 g (1½ oz) salt
10 g (⅓ oz) MSG

METHOD

Combine all of the ingredients and stir until the salt and MSG dissolve. (This is quickest if the dashi is warm.)

PER BOWL

≈30–45 ml (2–3 tbsp) shio tare
1–2 tsp melted lard or chicken fat
300 ml (10 fl oz/1¼ cups) Chintan Broth (page 229)
Hakodate-Style Noodles (page 233)
spring onions (scallions), thinly sliced
Chāshū, any cut (page 230)

OPTIONAL TOPPINGS

nori
menma
cress
grated fresh ginger root
fu (wheat gluten cakes)
pepper or ichimi
chilli oil
shellfish or sea vegetables (see below)

Prepare, cook and serve according to the guide on page 150.

VARIATIONS: KAISEN/KAISŌ SHIO RAMEN

Another unofficial Hokkaido ramen style is kaisen (seafood) ramen, typically a shio ramen adorned with seafood. All manner of shellfish are common, but personally I like clams, crab and squid best. Making kaisen ramen is easy – simply poach the seafood in the broth, then plonk it on top of the bowl.

A similar variant is *kaisō* ramen, made with sea vegetables. My favourite is *kirikonbu*, fresh kombu that's been finely shredded. Wakame, iwanori, tororo kombu, mekabu and mozuku are also excellent. These should be prepared (rehydrated and/or cooked if necessary) before adding them to the bowl.

ASAHIKAWA

旭
川

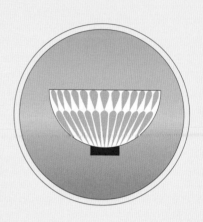

ASAPPY

© Asahikawa City

MASCOT: ASAPPY

Asappy, officially the 'Symbol Character of Asahikawa City': a seal who transformed into a polar bear, as he'd always dreamed of. He wears trousers with blue stripes to represent Asahikawa's many rivers, a belt in the form of the Asahi Bridge, and ramen noodle fringes on his sleeves. His name is a portmanteau of Asahikawa and 'happy.'

POPULATION: 320,437

ETYMOLOGY

Literally 'rising sun river,' perhaps a reference to the confluence of several rivers in the area, to the east of previously established settlements. Possibly derived from a misunderstanding of the Ainu name *ciw pet* (wavy river) as *cup pet* (sun river). The 'rising sun' (*asahi*) aspect of the name is also a reference to the Empire of Japan.[44]

旭川

A
S
A
H
I
K
A
W
A

旭川

旭川

A
S
A
H
I
K
A
W
A

旭川

Hokkaido is often deployed as a setting in Japanese art and fiction which acts as a kind of shorthand for existential emptiness and solitude. In the abstract for his 1984 *Hokkaido* series, photographer Daidō Moriyama wrote:

> I grabbed my camera every morning and took to the streets, with the regularity of an office worker, and no intention to meet any friend or acquaintance. I spent most of these three months on my own ... I soon ran out of sleeping pills, and as I didn't drink, all I could do was spend the long nights reading books. The daily photo shootings weren't really fruitful, and there I was, sitting in my freezing apartment, at my wit's end with my progressing mix of depersonalization, aphasia and insomnia...
>
> My lifestyle was from the very onset based on that fawning, illusional idea of escape and isolation; my only justification – taking photographs – was easily reversed from the true intention that it used to be, to mere pretense.[45]

Several works by Haruki Murakami similarly depict Hokkaido as a kind of disorienting, nondescript wasteland, and he singles out poor Asahikawa multiple times as particularly devoid of character and charm. *The Wind-Up Bird Chronicle* contains the brutal observation that 'No one wants to die in agony of ruptured internal organs in a blizzard in Asahikawa',[46] and one of the main characters in *Norwegian Wood* remarks, 'I finally get my freedom back and I'm supposed to go to Asahikawa? It's hard to get excited about a place like that – some hole in the ground.'[47]

Pretty harsh, Haruki! And yet ... maybe not such an unpopular opinion? A friend of mine described Asahikawa as a 'one horse town trying to keep itself amused' while Florentyna Leow notes that the city centre has 'a delightful and unapologetic air of sleaze about it' while also being 'prosaic'.[48] The blog *Murakami Pilgrimage* offers this appraisal: 'The city was a major industrial centre during World War II and today is known for its lumber industry and its large zoo. This made me somewhat skeptical... chances are that a city known primarily for its zoo isn't usually much to write home about.' In other words: exactly the kind of boring, generic setting that Murakami is trying to invoke.

→

But here's the thing: maybe Asahikawa is secretly kind of cool, precisely *because* it's boring? It feels like a place with nothing to prove. It doesn't have much to offer tourists, because it doesn't need to. Asahikawa just does its own thing, making wood into pulp and pulp into paper, turning off-cuts of pork into soothing soups and superlative drinking food.

Asahikawa draws in people and products from all corners of Hokkaido, connecting the island like a nerve centre, pulsing away with a quiet, consistent energy.

Or maybe I'm being too generous. Maybe Asahikawa actually is 'a singularly dull town', as Murakami puts it in *A Wild Sheep Chase*. To be honest, I found little to do there in between bowls of ramen. Then again, I don't know what to do in between bowls of ramen no matter where I am.

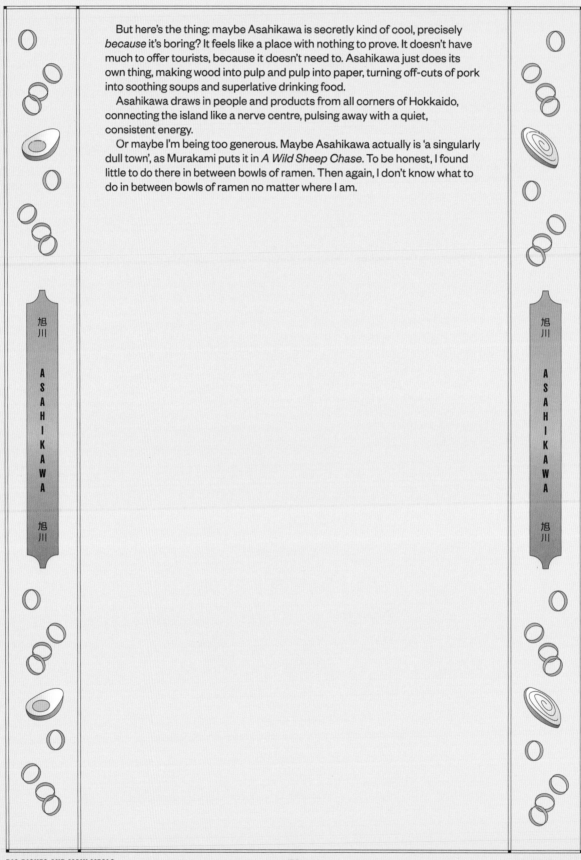

旭川

A
S
A
H
I
K
A
W
A

旭川

第 二 都 市

ASAHIKAWA SHŌYU RAMEN

ASAHIKAWA SHŌYU RĀMEN 旭川醤油ラーメン

If you forced me to name one ramen as 'the' ramen, a single bowl that could act as an exemplary version of the dish, it might be Asahikawa ramen. Why? First of all, it tends to be very well balanced – there's nothing intense or extreme about it. It's light enough that you can have three bowls in one day without feeling like dying (or at least I can), but it has enough lard in it to put meat on your bones. Asahikawa ramen also represents a perfect marriage of Chinese influence, Japanese flavours and local produce, an interplay that's key to ramen culture. It is known for establishing the 'double soup' technique, which uses two separate broths – one meat, one fish – which are then combined in the bowl. Asahikawa's position as a centre of food processing and distribution makes it a natural place for this style of ramen to have originated, as so much meat and seafood pass through the city.

Of course, the other thing that makes it a good representative of ramen generally is that there are limitless variations even within the framework of the style. (It doesn't even have to be soy sauce-based – that's just the most popular option.)

This recipe is inspired by Aoba and Tenkin, two old-school, no-frills shops that still command queues of both locals and tourists after decades of steadfast dedication to their craft.

PER BOWL
≈45 ml (3 tbsp) Shōyu Tare (page 230)
15–20 ml (3–4 tsp) hot, melted lard
200 ml (7 fl oz/scant 1 cup) Dōbutsu-Kei Broth (page 229)
100 ml (3½ fl oz/scant ½ cup) Kezuribushi (Dried Fish) Dashi (page 242) – saba, aji and niboshi are ideal for this
Asahikawa-Style Noodles (page 234)
spring onions (scallions)
menma
Chāshū, any cut (page 242)

OPTIONAL TOPPINGS
nori
grated fresh ginger root
ichimi

METHOD
Prepare, cook and serve according to the guide on page 150.

(SPICY) ASAHIKAWA OFFAL RAMEN

ASAHIKAWA HORUMON RĀMEN (GEKIKARAI NO) 旭川ホルモンラーメン（激辛いの）

In addition to the iconic double-soup shōyu ramen, Asahikawa has at least two other unique types of ramen. The best known outside of Asahikawa is probably Ramen Santōka, a shop specialising in a light tonkotsu-shio style topped with a tiny umeboshi, which has now become a huge international chain. But personally, I find another local ramen, *morumen*, far more compelling. It is a combination of ramen with another regional speciality, horumon (offal). Why is it not called *horumen*? I cannot find an answer. But essentially, it is an animal broth-based ramen – which can be shōyu, miso or shio – topped with stir-fried pig tripe or intestines (horumon). While not completely unique to Asahikawa, it makes sense here, as the city has historically always been a major site of meat processing. The original morumen shop, which has trademarked the term, is Himawari, operated by the Asaka family since the 1980s.

Morumen/horumon ramen is special to me because I used to make something similar for myself at my restaurant. We had horumon-yaki (grilled offal) on the menu, and a shōyu ramen – I would simply put the two together. I personally like my offal spicy, so this recipe is inspired by the '*gekikarai no*' miso morumen at Himawari. Simply leave the chilli elements out if you want a plainer ramen.

TRIPE - ENOUGH FOR 4 BOWLS

300 g (10½ oz) pork stomach or intestines
4 tbsp sake
2 tbsp vinegar
thumb-sized piece of fresh ginger root, thinly sliced

METHOD

Cover the pork offal with water and bring to a rolling boil. Boil for 5 minutes, to draw out the blood and scum from the offal, then discard the water and rinse the offal well with fresh water. Trim the offal of any rough bits – you may actually find particles of food or dirt in the crevices, so make sure these are scrupulously removed. Once the offal is cleaned, cut it into bite-size pieces and return to the pan along with the sake, vinegar, ginger and enough water to cover by a couple of inches.

Bring the water to a rolling boil and sustain for 3 hours, topping it up as needed. At this point the offal should be tender – soft but not so soft that it has no chew at all. Drain well, discard the ginger, and keep in the refrigerator until ready to use.

PER BOWL

a knob of lard
5–6 pieces boiled tripe (opposite)
a handful of bean sprouts, thinly sliced onions
    and carrots, chopped cabbage and nira,
    and rehydrated kikurage
1 tbsp gochujang
≈50 g (1¾ oz) Miso Tare (page)
300 ml (10 fl oz/1¼ cups) Dōbutsu-Kei Broth (page 229)
Asahikawa-Style Noodles (page 234)
≈1 tbsp spicy chilli oil
menma
spring onions (scallions)
about 1 tbsp gochugaru or similar coarse
    chilli powder/flakes
a handful of thread-cut chilli

METHOD

Add the lard to a wok and place over a very high heat. Once the fat is smoking, add the cooked offal, then the vegetables, and let them sit in the wok without stirring for about a minute, so they develop a strong char. Stir-fry everything for a couple minutes more, then add the gochujang and miso tare, and let them caramelise briefly. Pour in the broth and stir well. Cook the noodles as the broth comes to the boil. Drain the noodles and tip them into the bowl along with the chilli oil, then pour over the broth and stir-fried vegetables. Garnish with the menma, spring onions, chilli flakes and chilli threads.

KUSHIRO RAMEN

KUSHIRO RAMEN 釧路ラーメン

Kushiro ramen is promoted as the 'fourth ramen' of Hokkaido, though its history goes back almost as far as Hakodate's. Ramen based on Kantō-style 'Chinese soba' was first served in Kushiro in the Taishō period after being introduced by a chef from Yokohama,[49] and new ramen stalls thrived during reconstruction of the city following World War II. Kushiro ramen's incredibly simple, stripped-back character meant that it could be sold for a very, very low price – perfect for a defeated, down-on-their-luck populace.

Kushiro ramen is characterised by a light soy sauce-seasoned broth, strongly flavoured with katsuobushi, dosed with a generous amount of hot lard, which gives it a rich, meaty flavour. The most unique feature of Kushiro ramen is its noodles, which are very thin, but also curly and tender – highly slurpable and easy to chew. It is said that the thin noodles were made for busy fishermen and dock workers who didn't have a lot of time for lunch, so they demanded noodles that could be cooked and eaten quickly.

But to be honest this sort of theory always sounds like fakelore to me – like, how busy were these workers, exactly? Even quite thick noodles only take a few minutes to boil.

Whatever the reason, it remains a firm local favourite; Kushiro currently boasts 130 ramen shops. This particular recipe is based on the classic, simple version served at Kawamura.

PER BOWL

≈45 ml (3 tbsp) Shōyu Tare (page 230)
30 ml (2 tbsp) hot, melted lard
300 ml (10 fl oz/1¼ cups) Kushiro-style broth (see method)
Kushiro-Style Noodles (page 234)
spring onions (scallions)
menma
Loin Chāshū (page 230)

OPTIONAL TOPPINGS

black pepper
ichimi chilli
ajitama

METHOD

To make the broth, you will need 20 g (¾ oz) katsuobushi and 5 g (¼ oz) kombu per litre of chintan broth (page 229), to yield 900 ml (30½ fl oz/3¾ cups) – enough for three bowls, so increase this amount as needed. Add them after the broth has finished cooking and has been sieved, allowing them to infuse over a few hours as the broth cools; or you can do this in reverse, buy adding the katsuobushi and kombu to already chilled broth, letting it soak for as long as you like, then infusing as you reheat the broth (but do not boil them).

Once the dashi elements have infused, pass the broth through a sieve again before proceeding to make the ramen. Prepare, cook and serve according to the guide on page 150.

MURORAN/TOMAKOMAI CURRY RAMEN

MURORAN/TOMAKOMAI KARĒ RAMEN 室蘭・苫小牧カレーラーメン

It was only a matter of time before somebody combined ramen with curry, another one of the country's favourite comfort foods, and that's exactly what the proprietors of Aji no Daiō did in 1965, creating a fifth shining star in the constellation of Hokkaido ramen.

Curry ramen was invented by chef Ichirō Takahashi at his shop, Aji no Daiō, in Tomakomai, as a special designed to have broad, nostalgic[50] appeal to customers. In 1967 the Takahashi family relocated to Iwamizawa and opened a new shop there, where a loyal customer named Hiroshi Koyanagi became so enamoured with their miso and curry ramen that he became an apprentice to learn their recipes.

In 1972, Koyanagi went on to open his own branch of Aji no Daiō in Muroran, capitalising on the manufacturing town's hordes of hungry factory workers.[51] The Koyanagi branch of the business would become a small chain across southern Hokkaido.[52] Meanwhile, the Takahashi family returned to Tomakomai and opened their own Aji no Daiō there, which now has multiple branches as well.[53] Both towns justifiably claim curry ramen as their own. However, it is more commonly associated with Muroran, partially because of a 1999 endorsement of Aji no Daiō's Muroran main store by Muroran native Natsumi Abe, a member of the perennially popular idol group Morning Musume.[54]

Over the years, dozens of imitators have opened, but Aji no Daiō's flagship in Muroran still boasts sizeable queues and an impressive collection of celebrity autographs on the walls. The accolades are well deserved.

Truly, their curry ramen is one of the greatest bowls I have ever had, a revelation – which, after all these years, after so much ramen, is quite a feat. I saw the face of God in that bowl.

This recipe is as close as I've gotten to recreating it. Of course, every curry ramen shop does things a little differently, so with that in mind, feel free to adjust this however you like. You could make a decent version by just making a good miso (pages 151–152) or shōyu (page 160) ramen and adding a cube of curry roux to it. But ramen is something that rewards a bit of effort, so you may as well do it properly. This recipe has been adapted from *Ramen Forever*.

MAKES AROUND 500 G/1 LB 2 OZ, ENOUGH FOR 10 BOWLS

CURRY PASTE

4 tbsp (20 g/¾ oz) Madras curry powder
   (hot or mild or a mix of both)
3 tbsp (15 g/½ oz) garam masala
1 tsp Chinese five spice powder
50 g (1¾ oz) lard
120 g (4¼ oz) onion (1 medium), peeled and finely diced
80 g (2¾ oz) sweet potato, peeled and coarsely grated
15 g (½ oz) fresh ginger root, washed and thinly sliced
6 garlic cloves, thinly sliced
30 g (1 oz) tomato purée (paste)
200 ml (7 fl oz/scant 1 cup) water
4 tbsp tonkatsu sauce
4 tbsp shōyu
1 teaspoon cornflour (cornstarch)

METHOD

Blitz all of the spices in a spice grinder for a minute
– these should be finely ground, or the finished curry will
be too grainy. Melt the lard in a saucepan over a medium
heat and add the onion. Cook until well browned, then
add the sweet potato, ginger and garlic, and cook for
a few more minutes until they soften. Stir in the tomato
purée, and cook for another few minutes. Add the spices
along with about a quarter of the water and bring to
a boil, stirring well as it heats up. Add the remaining water
and boil for 10 minutes. In a small bowl, stir together the
tonkatsu sauce, shōyu and cornflour until no lumps of
cornflour remain, then pour this into the curry liquid,
stir well, and continue boiling for another few minutes.
Remove from the heat and blitz the tare until smooth
with a stick blender or food processor. Leave to cool,
then keep in the refrigerator (for up to a week) or freezer
(indefinitely) until ready to use.

PER BOWL

a handful of bean sprouts
≈50 g (1¾ oz) curry paste
1 tbsp lard
≈30 ml (2 tbsp) Shōyu Tare (page 230) or ≈50 g (1¾ oz)
   Miso Tare (page 152)
300 ml (10 fl oz/1¼ cups) Dōbutsu-Kei Broth (page 229)
Sapporo-Style Noodles (page 233)
1 tsp dried wakame, rehydrated
Chāshū, made from shoulder meat (page 230)
spring onions (scallions)
menma (optional)

METHOD

Briefly stir-fry the bean sprouts and curry paste with
the lard in a wok set over a high heat before adding the
tare and the broth. Boil the broth for a couple of minutes,
then cook and drain the noodles and tip into a bowl.
Pour over the broth and bean sprouts, then garnish
with the wakame, chāshū, spring onions and menma
(if using).

旨さが濃いから
あとをひく
またすぐに
食べたくなる
ああこの味が
ふるさと
旭川なんだ

PORK CUTLET SPAGHETTI

SUPAKATSU スパカツ

The yōshoku restaurant Izumiya in Kushiro has been in business since 1959 and its claim to fame is the glorious *spa-katsu*, short for *spa*ghetti ton*katsu*, a fried pork chop piled onto spaghetti with meat sauce, served on a sizzling hotplate. When it arrived at my table, an easy listening version of 'Bali Ha'i' was playing on the restaurant's speakers – a fitting soundtrack for this dramatic, volcanic mountain of food.

SERVES 2, QUITE GENEROUSLY

2 pork loin steaks
salt and pepper, as needed
½ batch Pané Batter (page 91)
about 50 g (1¾ oz) panko
oil, for deep-frying
200 g (7 oz) spaghetti
400 ml (14 fl oz/generous 1½ cups) Meat Sauce
    (page 242), kept hot
Tabasco sauce and grated Parmesan,
    as needed (optional)

METHOD

Season both sides of each pork steak with salt and pepper, then dredge in the batter, then the panko. Heat the oil in a wide pan to 180°C (360°F) and bring a pot of water to the boil for the pasta. Cook the spaghetti until it's a slightly softer than al dente.

As the pasta cooks, lower the pork into the oil and cook for about 5–6 minutes, until nicely coloured and crisp on the outside, then remove and drain on a wire rack. By now the spaghetti should be just about cooked, but don't rush it – the pork needs to rest for a few minutes anyway. Slice the pork into 2.5 cm (1 in) thick pieces. Drain the pasta when it's done, then tip it into a lightly oiled frying pan set over a high heat. Add the sliced katsu on top of the spaghetti, then pour over the sauce. Let everything sizzle in the pan for a minute, then serve and enjoy piping hot, with as much Tabasco and Parmesan as you like.

SCALLOP AND ONION YAKISOBA

OHÔTSUKU KITAMI SHIO YAKISOBA オホーツク北見塩やきそば

The Kitami city government developed this dish in 2007 to promote local produce – namely onions, from the many farms that surround Kitami, and scallops, from the nearby Sea of Okhotsk. And like so many of these invented local dishes, there are rules: the noodles must be made from Hokkaido wheat, it must be served on a sizzle plate, with chopsticks made from Hokkaido timber, and it should be served with a soup that also uses ingredients local to Kitami. Outside of Hokkaido it may not be possible to follow all of these rules. But we can take inspiration from it to make a delicious noodle dinner with the natural sweetness of scallops and onions.

SERVES 2

2 Cream Croquettes, using crab (page 93),
   plus oil for deep-frying (optional)
1 tbsp vegetable oil
150 g (5½ oz) scallops, patted dry on all sides
1 large or 2 small onions, cut with the grain
   into 1 cm (½ in) thick slices
a handful (about 50 g/1¾ oz) of shimeji mushrooms
1 small head (about 50 g/1¾ oz) of tatsoi or komatsuna,
   cut into 5 cm (2 in) pieces
a few slices of red (bell) pepper
many grinds of black pepper
2 portions of yakisoba noodles
a generous knob of butter
6 tbsp Shio Tare (page 155), or 1 tsp salt and
   ½ tsp kombu dashi powder dissolved into
   1 tbsp sake and 5 tbsp water
a handful of chives, finely sliced
a small handful of crispy fried onions

METHOD

If you are serving this with the croquettes, fry them according to the instructions on page 89 before starting the stir-fry, and keep them hot in a low oven.

Heat the vegetable oil in a large, non-stick frying pan or well-seasoned cast-iron pan over a high heat until it begins to smoke. Add the scallops and onions and stir-fry for a couple minutes until lightly browned, then add the mushrooms, tatsoi, red pepper and black pepper, and stir-fry for another 2–3 minutes until all of the vegetables are slightly charred but still crunchy. Add the noodles, butter and half of the tare, and stir-fry for another minute or two. Pour over the remaining tare and cook the noodles for a few minutes, without stirring, so they brown and crisp slightly on the bottom of the pan. Garnish with the chives, crispy onions and croquettes (if using). This is best eaten directly from the pan, so bring the whole thing to the table with side plates.

STIR-FRIED NOODLES WITH A VERY THICK SAUCE

CHĀMEN チャーメン・炒麺

Chāmen is a Wakkanai speciality similar to Otaru's *ankake yakisoba*, and Ashibetsu's gatatan (page 141). While the name chāmen – which just means 'stir-fried noodles' – does appear on restaurant menus in other parts of the country, such as the Chinatowns of Yokohama and Nagasaki, this particular version is unique to Wakkanai.[55] Its appeal is irresistible in such a windswept, snowy climate: the incredibly thick sauce (ankake) insulates the veg, noodles and shellfish beneath, like a heavy duvet. The generous portion size is a big selling point as well.

SERVES 2

3 tbsp oil
80 g (2¾ oz) pork, very thinly sliced (optional)
½ green (bell) pepper, cut into large chunks
½ Chinese leaf (napa cabbage), roughly chopped
½ carrot, peeled and cut into thin planks
a few pieces of kikurage, rehydrated and
    cut into large chunks
100 g (3½ oz) bean sprouts
150 g (5½ oz) shellfish – prawns (shrimp),
    scallops, squid, etc
400 ml (14 fl oz/generous 1½ cups) water
    or light broth
2 tbsp shōyu
2 tbsp sake
1 tbsp caster (superfine) sugar
1 tbsp oyster sauce
1 tbsp chicken powder
4 tbsp cornflour (cornstarch) or potato starch mixed
    with 6 tbsp cold water
white pepper, to taste
2 portions of ramen noodles, cooked and drained
chilli oil, beni shōga (red, julienned pickled ginger)
    and/or vinegar to garnish

METHOD

Pour half of the oil into a wok and set over a high heat. Stir-fry the pork (if using) until cooked through, then add the pepper, cabbage and carrot and stir-fry for a minute or two until the cabbage is wilted slightly. Add the kikurage, bean sprouts and shellfish and stir-fry for another minute, then add the water, soy sauce, sake, sugar, oyster sauce and chicken powder. Drizzle in the cornflour slurry, stir well, and bring to the boil. Add some white pepper, taste, and adjust the seasoning as you like.

Meanwhile, heat the remaining oil in a separate wok or non-stick pan over a high heat, and add the noodles, spreading them out in a layer that fills the pan. Start this around the time you add the vegetables to the other wok; the noodles should fry for about 5 minutes, to develop a crust. When the noodles are crisp, tip them out onto wide dishes and then ladle over the ankake. Serve very hot, with vinegar, chilli oil, and/or pickled ginger, to taste.

FRIED SALMON RICE BOWL

OHÔTSUKU ABASHIRI ZANGI-DON オホーツク網走ザンギ丼

In 2008, the Abashiri city government initiated a campaign for a new local speciality featuring Karafuto trout or, as it is locally branded, Okhotsk salmon. The new dish, of trout (or salmon) fried in the style of zangi, served on rice, was to be called Okhotsk Abashiri Zangi Don, and it had rules – so very many rules. (See also: Kitami yakisoba, page 172.) For the purposes of simply enjoying some tasty fried salmon at home, I think it is okay to break many of these rules, but there is at least one that I think should be adhered to, which is the use of fish sauce instead of soy sauce. This is said to preserve the colour of the fish, and it is, of course, another opportunity to use a unique local product. Japanese fish sauces (*gyoshō*) tend to be less intense than their Southeast Asian counterparts, so if you can't get actual Hokkaido fish sauce, I suggest a little *nam pla* or similar mixed with light Japanese soy sauce.

SERVES 2, PERHAPS 3 IF ONE PERSON IS NOT VERY HUNGRY

MARINATED SALMON
250–300 g (9–10½ oz) salmon, boneless and scaled and cut into chunks about 3 cm (1 in) thick
3 tbsp sake
2 tbsp gyoshō (Japanese fish sauce), or 1 tbsp each usukuchi shōyu and Southeast Asian fish sauce
⅛ tsp salt
⅛ tsp MSG
20 g (¾ oz) fresh ginger root, peeled and finely chopped
½ garlic clove, grated or finely chopped
a few pinches of finely ground white pepper

TO COOK AND SERVE
½ red onion, very thinly sliced
75 g (2½ oz/½ cup) potato starch
75 g (2½ oz/generous ½ cup) plain (all-purpose) flour
vegetable oil, for deep frying
    (about 1 litre/34 fl oz/4¼ cups)
2–3 portions of rice (cooked)
a small handful of pea shoots or cress
ponzu, grated horseradish and/or fresh lemon, cut into wedges, to serve

METHOD
Combine the salmon with all of the marinade ingredients and mix well, then refrigerate for 1–2 hours. Place the sliced onion in a bowl and cover with ice water, and leave for at least 20 minutes, to crisp them and soften their harsh, raw flavour.

To cook, combine the flours in a large bowl and mix well. Heat the oil in a deep, wide pan to 180°C (350°F). Dredge the marinated salmon in the flours, then lower each piece carefully into the oil, and cook for about 5–6 minutes, until golden brown. When the salmon is almost done, scoop the rice into bowls, then remove the salmon from the oil and drain on a rack or paper towel. Place the salmon on top of the rice, garnish with the sliced red onions and pea shoots or cress, and serve with ponzu, horseradish and/or lemon wedges (all to taste).

GRILLED PORK BOWL

OBIHIRO BUTADON 帯広豚丼

Butadon – pork bowl – is an Obihiro speciality which, like Muroran Yakitori (page 98), is an instance of pork acting as a substitute protein. Apparently, the founder of local restaurant Panchō, Shūji Abe, wanted to serve unagi (eel), but it was difficult to procure in Hokkaido. He tried the same dish – same tare, same technique – with local pork instead, and found it to be a delicious success. They even hung a banner outside boasting, 'better than unagi-don!'[56] I am tempted to agree – it's *really* good. The locals must agree, too; Panchō is still going strong after 90 years (!), and has inspired countless imitators.

The recipe that follows is for a single serving – just scale up as needed. Because the dish is so simple, ingredients and technique are of utmost importance. Which is to say: you must cook this over charcoal and use the best quality pork you can buy.

SERVES 1

200 g (7 oz) pork belly, rind removed,
    cut into slices about 5 mm (¼ in) thick
salt
100 ml (3½ fl oz/scant ½ cup) Pork Tare (page 243)
cooked rice – enough to fill a small-ish donburi
    (at least 100 g/3½ oz/1 cup uncooked weight)
a few green peas

OPTIONAL GARNISHES:
grated horseradish
butter
spring onions (scallions), very thinly sliced

METHOD

Lightly season the sliced pork belly with salt, have the rice hot and ready to go, and have the tare at room temperature. Prepare a barbecue with the coals positioned just a couple inches beneath a mesh grill plate. Cook the pork slices on each side for 2–3 minutes or so, or until lightly charred and just cooked through. Dunk the pork in the tare to coat each piece, then return to the barbecue and cook for another minute, then dunk again and cook for another minute. Transfer the pork onto bowls of rice, garnish with a few green peas, and place a lid or up-turned dish on top of the pork to keep everything hot before serving.

NOTE

You will not use the full amount of tare here, but you need this much volume in order to dip the pork into it.

RICE WITH MEAT SAUCE AND HOT DOGS
HOMAGE TO CALIFORNIA BABY

CALIFORNIA BABY NO SHISUKO RAISU NO OMĀJU カリフォルニアベイビーのシスコライスのオマージュ

Lucky Pierrot (pages 123–124) isn't the only place in Hakodate for new takes on American comfort food. There's also California Baby, a little slice of San Francisco in southern Hokkaido. The owner, Shūhei Shibata, was inspired to create this shrine to American diner culture after travelling in California in the 1970s, and the locals have appreciated the café's big flavours and big portions ever since. The signature dish of hot dogs, meat sauce and rice – 'Sisco Rice' – has even been called 'the taste of Hakodateites' youth'.[57] It is easy to love; the meat sauce acts like a mild chilli con carne, a perfect condiment for the smoky, snappy franks.

SERVES 2

300 ml (10 fl oz/1¼ cups) Meat Sauce (page 242)
a knob of butter
2 large portions of rice, cooked
4 smoky, coarsely-ground hot dogs
   (Polish sausages work well), skin scored
a few broccoli florets, boiled or steamed
2 spoonfuls of sweetcorn
2 scoops of potato salad (optional)
2 dollops of mayo (optional)
hot sauce, to taste (optional)

METHOD

Reheat the meat sauce and keep it hot, then fold the butter through the hot rice. Cook the hot dogs as you like – for this I prefer them boiled. Dish the rice out onto plates, place the hot dogs on top of the rice, then ladle the meat sauce all over. Garnish with the broccoli, corn and, if you like, potato salad and mayo. Serve with hot sauce on the side.

SURF CLAM RICE BENTO

BOKOI MESHI NO OMĀJU 母恋めしのオマージュ

Bokoi meshi is a famous bento from Bokoi Station, in Muroran; the area's name is thought to be a corruption of the Ainu *pok o i*, meaning 'place where clams grow', and the kanji transliteration means 'mother's love'. In most cases in Hokkaido, kanji used for place names is meaningless, but in Bokoi it may have a connection to a local Ainu legend.[58] There was once an elderly couple who went to forage for food in the bay, to help hungry people in their kotan. They were killed by a god who lived in the water, who thought they had come looking for his treasure. When the couple didn't come back to the village, their daughter set out to find them, searching tirelessly for days. Finally she encountered the god, who listened to her story and realised his terrible mistake. As atonement, he filled the bay with clams for the villagers. The area is said to have gotten its kanji name in reference to the devotion the daughter showed towards her parents, and the area is still blessed with an abundance of surf clams.

SERVES 2

400 ml (14 fl oz/1⅔ cup) water
10 g (⅓ oz) kombu
60 g (2 oz) surf clam meat (or meat from similar large clams)
2 tbsp sake
1 tbsp usukuchi shōyu
1 tbsp mirin
1 tbsp sugar
250 g (9 oz/1⅛ cup) rice (washed)

OPTIONAL SIDES

2 smoked eggs
2 pieces of *kukiwakame/otsumami wakame* ('snack' wakame)
2 pieces of smoked cheese
2 spoonfuls of aubergine (eggplant) pickles (such as *shiba-zuke*)
4 mints (individually wrapped)

METHOD

Combine the water and kombu in a saucepan and soak for at least 2 hours, then bring to the boil. Sustain at a low boil for 10 minutes, then add the clam meat and boil for another 10 minutes. Remove from the heat and leave to cool slightly. Retrieve the kombu and clams from the dashi. Cut three or four strips from the kombu, about 1 cm (½ in) wide, then cut across these strips into very small shreds. Set aside four of the largest, most attractive pieces of clam, and coarsely chop the rest.

Pour the clam-katsuo dashi into a measuring jug and add the sake, shōyu, mirin and sugar. If necessary, top up with water so the total amount of liquid is 375 ml (12⅔ fl oz/scant 1⅔ cups). Tip this into a rice cooker or saucepan along with the rice, chopped clam meat and shredded kombu, and stir. Cut each of the reserved pieces of clam in half lengthways, then place these on top of the rice and cook according to the instructions on page 243. When the rice is done, remove the large pieces of clam from the top and set aside, then mix the rice well. Leave to cool slightly, then form into four onigiri, with the reserved clam pieces pressed into their surface.

The rice can be enjoyed as part of any Japanese meal, but to make the complete Bokoi meshi-style bento, wrap the onigiri in cling film (plastic wrap) and pack into a bento along with all of the side items.

CHOOSE-YOUR-OWN SASHIMI BOWL

KATTE-DON 勝手丼

One of Hokkaido's most iconic dishes is kaisendon, or seafood rice bowls, and some of the best kaisendon come from Washō Market in Kushiro. There, the dish is sold for breakfast and called *katte-don*, which translates roughly as 'your-own-way bowl'. You buy a bowl of hot rice, then take it to a fishmonger's counter and choose from dozens of varieties of impeccably fresh fish, laid out in chilled display cabinets, like jewels in a pawn shop window.

As long as you can source some fantastic fish, it's not hard to recreate a similarly delicious sashimi bowl at home.

PER BOWL

1 portion of warm, freshly cooked rice
(75–125 g/2½–4½ oz/⅓–generous ½ cup uncooked)
about 150–200 g (5½–7 oz) sashimi grade seafood –
the very best quality you can source
shōyu, wasabi and *gari,* thinly sliced pickled ginger
(to taste)

METHOD

The method here hardly needs to be explained: arrange fish attractively on rice; enjoy with soy sauce, wasabi and gari. But there are some finer points to keep in mind. One is the temperature of the rice; it should be just hot enough to draw out the oils of the fish, without making it noticeably warm.

Another point is to use a variety of fish and shellfish to enjoy a wide range of textures and flavours. Go for a mix of white and darker-fleshed fish, leaner cuts and fattier ones, as well as some choice crustaceans, molluscs and roe – for me, no kaisendon is complete without crab, ikura and perhaps some uni.

SOUP CURRY

SŪPU KARĒ スープカレー

Soup curry is popular across Hokkaido, but it is most strongly associated with Sapporo, where it originated in the 1970s at a restaurant called Ajanta. Ajanta's founder, Muneo Tatsujiri, was initially inspired to start making curry on a trip to India, where he discovered that many of the same spices used in Indian recipes also featured in traditional Chinese medicine. He began making his own *yakuzen karī* ('medicinal curry') broth in 1971, but it was customer requests that created what we now know as soup curry.

Tatsujiri's medicinal soup was based on chicken and vegetables, and these ingredients would then be thrown away at the end of the boil. But hungry customers looking for a good deal began to ask Tatsujiri if they could eat the boiled meat and veg instead, and he obliged. The off-menu, hearty soup caught on, and over the years it was refined, to add more ingredients and cook them with more care. Dozens of imitators followed, and Sapporo now has over 200 dedicated soup curry shops.[59]

Soup curry contains a variety of vegetables, cooked *suage* or 'plain-fried' in oil, without batter or breading. It also features a highly complex masala, unique to each shop. Ajanta, for example, uses 30 different spices plus 15 medicinal herbs!

A healthy eating ethos remains a consideration not only at Ajanta but at many other soup curry shops, which choose both spices and vegetables for their health benefits in addition to their flavour. To honour this tradition, I have included a few mood- and energy-boosting ingredients, such as ginseng, ashwagandha and – as a nod to Furano – a bit of lavender. But soup curry is customisable, so use whatever spices you prefer. Similarly, if the suage frying process is too tedious, the vegetables can be roasted instead.

SERVES 4

SOUP

2 tbsp vegetable oil
2 whole chicken legs, cut into thighs and drumsticks
1 onion, coarsely chopped
1 carrot, coarsely chopped
4 garlic cloves, chopped
2 cm (¾ in) piece fresh ginger root, peeled and chopped
8 fresh curry leaves (optional)
2 tbsp fresh or frozen methi leaves (optional)
40 g (1½ oz) soup curry masala (page 188),
    or a spice mix of your choosing
4 tbsp tomato purée (paste)
1.5 litres (52 fl oz/6¼ cups) water
15–20 g (½–¾ oz) kombu
2 dried shiitake (about 5 g/⅛ oz total)
2 tbsp good quality mango chutney
½ tsp salt (or more or less, to taste)

METHOD

Set the oil over a high heat in a casserole and add the chicken legs. Brown on all sides, then remove from the pan and lower the heat to medium. Add the onion, carrot, garlic, ginger, curry leaves and methi leaves (if using). Sauté for a few minutes until the vegetables are browned, then add the masala, tomato purée and stir well. Cook the spices for a minute or two, then add the water and return the chicken to the pan, and add the kombu, shiitake, mango chutney and salt. Simmer with a lid on the pot for 1 hour until the chicken is pulling away from the bone. Remove the chicken carefully so that it does not break apart, and set aside to cool. Remove the kombu, shiitake and star anise and discard, then blend the remaining ingredients into the broth with a stick blender. Pass the broth through a sieve, then taste and adjust seasoning as you like.

TOPPINGS AND SIDES

300 g (10½ oz/1½ cups) rice
¼ tsp ground turmeric or 5–6 saffron threads
a small knob of butter
4 pieces of each of 8–12 different vegetables –
    choose what's in season and what you like; some
    of my favourites are squash, (bell) peppers, aubergine
    (eggplant), baby corn, oyster mushrooms, okra, snap
    peas, asparagus, beetroot (beets) and lotus root
cooked and chilled chicken (see above)
about 1.5 litres (52 fl oz/6¼ cups) vegetable oil,
    for deep-frying
salt, to taste

METHOD

Combine the rice, turmeric, butter and water in
a saucepan or rice cooker and cook according to
the instructions on page xx. Cut the vegetables into
sizes that will cook fairly quickly – squash should be
cut into quite thin slices, lotus root into 5 mm (¼ in)
slices, and peppers and aubergines into big chunks,
etc. Mushrooms, okra, snap peas and the like can be
left whole.

Turn the oven on to 60°C (140°F) – you will use this
to keep things warm as you cook. Heat the oil in a wide
pan to 180°C (350°F), then fry the vegetables in batches,
so they cook in a single layer (otherwise they will steam
rather than fry). Cook each veg until done – an annoying
instruction, I know, but each one needs to be fried for
a different amount of time. For example peppers will only
take a minute; squash will take more like 4–5 minutes.
Use your own judgement here.

Drain the cooked vegetables on a wire rack and
season with a pinch of salt. Transfer to the oven to keep
warm while you finish cooking. Continue until all the veg
are cooked and seasoned, then fry the chicken until
evenly browned.

To serve, ladle the hot soup into bowls and top
with the fried vegetables. Serve with rice and fried
chicken on the side.

MASALA

seeds from 4 cardamom pods
4 whole cloves
2 dried bay leaves
1 tbsp coriander seeds
1 tbsp cumin seeds
1 tsp black peppercorns
1 tsp fennel seeds
1 tsp caraway seeds
½ tsp fenugreek seeds
1 tsp black mustard seeds
1 star anise
¼ tsp lavender buds
1 tbsp ground turmeric
2 tsp gochugaru or similar coarse chilli powder
    (or more, to taste)
1 tsp nigella seeds
1 tsp ground cinnamon
½ tsp ground ginger
¼ tsp ground mace
¼ tsp ashwagandha powder
¼ tsp ginseng powder
¼ tsp dried sage
¼ tsp dried thyme
¼ tsp sanshō
¼ tsp smoked paprika
⅛ tsp Kashmiri (or similar) chilli powder
⅛ tsp jalapeño powder or similar
⅛ tsp asafoetida

METHOD

Place the cardamom, cloves, bay, coriander, cumin,
peppercorns, fennel, caraway, fenugreek, mustard and
star anise in a frying pan and set over a medium heat.
Toast the spices, stirring often until they are slightly
darker in colour, then tip them out of the pan and leave
to cool. Remove the star anise and set it aside; this will
go in whole. Grind the rest of the toasted spices and the
lavender buds to a powder in a spice grinder. Combine
with all of the remaining spices and mix well.

少年よ、大志を抱け！

SWE

お菓子・パ

FURANO

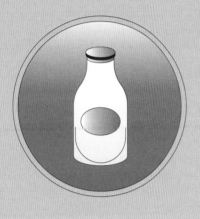

富良野

HESOMARU

MASCOT: HESOMARU

Hesomaru, who represents Furano's annual Belly Button Festival, held because Furano is the 'belly button', or geographic centre, of Hokkaido. Hesomaru is obsessed with navels, has a belly button for a nose, and also kind of is a belly button (?).

ETYMOLOGY

From the Ainu *hura nuy*, 'stinky flame'. Likely a reference to sulfuric springs near Mount Tokachi. The kanji transliteration means 'prosperous, good plains'.

POPULATION: 19,949

© Hokkai Heso Matsuri Executive Committee

Summer in Hokkaido is as green as the winter is white. As the snow melts, seedlings burst forth, and the plains and valleys become silly with chlorophyll, bright as a glass of genmaicha.

The melting snow creates another colour, too: rust. Coarse patches of brownish orange break out on barns, bridges, tractors, bicycles, factories, silos, hotels, bathhouses – everywhere.

But green and rust-red aren't Hokkaido's most famous colours. If you've Googled Hokkaido even once, you've probably seen the technicolor flower fields of Furano, candy stripes across the rolling hills, like something by Van Gogh. Furano and nearby Biei are full of these fields, none more famous than Farm Tomita, which has been operating since 1953, and has been a destination for photographers and tourists since the 1970s.

Today, I am one of those tourists. I put on a floral print shirt and I pile onto the seasonal train to the makeshift 'Lavender Farm Station,' just some scaffolding along the tracks. The train is buzzing with excitement; I overhear conversations in Japanese, Chinese, Korean, English and Thai. Everyone is taking videos, taking selfies, chatting happily, eating ice cream at 10am. I'm not the only one wearing a floral print.

Tourists – and tourism, generally – gets a bad rap. *'Don't be a tourist',* they say. But why? I looked around, and I thought, *these people are having the time of their lives. They've probably been looking forward to this for months. They will always remember this and they have each other to enjoy it with.* Would they gain anything from trying to blend in and 'go where the locals go', by *not* seeing the beautiful flowers at the farm, *not* eating the melon, *not* having an ice cream, not taking photos and not generally making the most of their brief time on this earth?

In *The Philosophy of the Tourist*, Hiroki Azuma offers a defence of tourism as something that 'brings the universal and particular together without the condition of belonging to a state',[60] and he admires tourists for a number of reasons. They make a concerted effort to experience things beyond their everyday lives. They ignore national boundaries as the artificial constructs that they are. They meet other people outside of their own culture with nonchalant indifference. They spend money in economies that are not their own.

Azuma even thinks of tourism as a kind of diplomacy. He argues that people who visit other countries are '*contributing to peace independently of the state system* ... For example, relations between Japan and China or Japan and Korea have always involved serious political issues, but the deterioration of the situation has been significantly limited by the massive number of tourists that travel between the countries.'[61] Azuma's perspective is the inverse of how I had always perceived tourism, which is that it is enabled by the state in order to maintain goodwill between citizens, not the other way around.

Don't get me wrong: sometimes, tourism still sucks. In places like Kyoto or Rome, it's way out of hand. I might even go so far to say it's basically ruined those places. You go to the Golden Pavilion and the power and beauty of the experience is destroyed by the sheer number of people there, all jockeying for position to get a selfie. This kind of tourism – going places unthinkingly just because those are the places you're meant to go – is kind of awful.

Besides, herding people towards the same old sites takes them away from other places that just as wondrous and fascinating. And many of these places *need* tourists, too – economies and livelihoods rely on them. I guess it might be hard to get people to go places like Ashibetsu or Tokachi-Shimizu. On the other hand, isn't a bowl of gatatan or a teishoku of local beef, for many, just as enjoyable, just as resonant, as museums or monuments? Personally, I'd take the flower fields and fruit pastries of Furano over the temples and tea of Kyoto any day.

During peak season, Farm Tomita is already pretty crowded, and I suppose there is a risk that Hokkaido could become just as oversubscribed as Kyoto. Maybe, to some people, it already is. But moderate levels of tourism is no bad thing, for both the tourists and for their destinations. Writing for *The Atlantic*, Jerusalem Desmas puts it quite well: 'Tourists are like bees: I don't want a bunch of them circling around me, but I also don't want them to disappear... Show me a city without tourists, and I'll show you a city in decline.'[62] How many times have you actually been stung by a bee, anyway?

観光客の哲学

FRESH MILK ICE CREAM

SEINYŪ AISU 生乳アイス

One of the finest ways to enjoy the flavour of Hokkaido milk is to churn it into ice cream. This recipe doubles down on the milkiness of milk by using milk powder and condensed milk, but you should also use the most delicious, freshest milk you can. Unpasteurised milk is particularly flavourful.

**MAKES ABOUT 500 ML
(17 FL OZ/GENEROUS 2 CUPS)**

4 egg yolks
⅛ tsp cornflour
30 g (1 oz) caster (superfine) sugar
10 g (⅓ oz) milk powder
120 g (4¼ oz) condensed milk
100 ml (3½ fl oz/scant ½ cup) double (heavy) cream, the best quality you can buy
250 ml (8 fl oz/1 cup) whole, very fresh, very good quality milk (ideally unhomogenised and unpasteurised)
a pinch of salt

METHOD

In a bowl or large jug, whisk the egg yolks, cornflour and sugar until smooth. Combine the remaining ingredients in a saucepan and whisk well. Set over a medium heat and bring to the boil, stirring very frequently with a spatula, scraping the sides and bottom of the pan as you go. As soon as the mixture boils and foams up, switch off the heat. When the bubbling subsides, steadily pour into the egg yolks, whisking constantly until smooth and well mixed. Return to the pan, then bring to a bare simmer while stirring constantly with a spatula. Leave to cool, then transfer to the refrigerator and chill completely before churning into ice cream according to your ice-cream maker's instructions.

VARIATIONS

The options for ice cream in Hokkaido don't stop at delicious fresh milk. You will find anything from kombu to kabocha, plus the iconic melon and lavender. I even saw butadon (page 178) ice cream advertised in Obihiro. Hokkaido is an ice cream wonderland.

CHEESE: Replace the cream with 100 g (3½ oz) cream cheese or mascarpone, but whisk it into the custard base after it has been cooked, to prevent curdling.

MELON: Increase the cornflour (cornstarch) to ¼ teaspoon, and replace 125 ml (4¼ fl oz/½ cup) of the milk with 125 g (4½ oz) of cantaloupe purée. Don't cook it, just blend it until smooth, then whisk it into the cooked custard mixture after it has been combined with the egg yolks. Pass the finished melon custard through a fine sieve, then add a little bit of orange food colouring, and if your melon is not tasty enough, add a dash of melon essence.

LAVENDER: Add 1 tbsp of dried lavender buds to the milk mixture at the beginning of cooking. Pass the liquid through a sieve after mixing with the yolks. Add enough food colouring to make it a lovely lavender colour. You can also replace some or all of the condensed milk with honey.

MELON CREAM PUFF

MERON SHŪ KURĪMU メロンシュークリーム

This is a simple, melony take on the classic cream puff, with a melon-flavoured custard as well as little chunks of fresh melon adorning the whipped cream. I prefer to eat this with my hands, which takes you on a journey: first you get the fresh melon, then the whipped cream, and finally, the melon custard, which unites the layers in a satisfying melon denouement.

MAKES 6 PUFFS

MELON CUSTARD
½ teaspoon vanilla extract or paste
60 g (2 oz/generous ¼ cup) caster (superfine) sugar
2 egg yolks
10 g (⅓ oz/1½ tbsp) cornflour (cornstarch)
7 g (¼ oz/1 tbsp) plain (all-purpose) flour
120 ml (4 fl oz/½ cup) whole milk
120 g (4¼ oz) very good, very ripe cantaloupe
orange food colouring and melon essence,
    as needed (optional)

CHOUX
50 g (1¾ oz) butter
a pinch of salt
60 ml (2 fl oz/¼ cup) water
60 ml (2 fl oz/¼ cup) milk
75 g (2½ oz/generous ½ cup) plain (all-purpose) flour
2 eggs
sprinkles or pearl sugar, as needed

TO ASSEMBLE
200 ml (7 fl oz/scant 1 cup) whipping cream
2 tbsp icing (powdered) sugar
1 tsp vanilla extract
about 120 g (4¼ oz) cantaloupe, coarsely chopped

METHOD
For the melon custard, whisk together the vanilla, sugar, yolks and flours in a medium, microwave-safe bowl to make a coarse paste. Whisk in a splash of milk, to thin the yolk mixture, then the rest of it, little by little, until smooth. Blend the cantaloupe to a smooth purée, then pass it through a sieve into the milk mixture, and stir well. Microwave on full power (800W), uncovered, for 3 minutes, whisking well after each minute. Leave to cool slightly, then taste the custard; if you like, enhance its flavour and colour with some melon essence and food colouring. Cover with a piece of parchment placed directly on the surface of the custard. Transfer to the refrigerator to chill completely. When the custard is cold, transfer to a piping bag.

Make the choux by combining the butter, salt, water and milk in a saucepan and bring to a simmer. Remove from the heat, then beat in the flour. Place the pan back on a medium heat and stir for a few minutes until it dries out slightly and reaches a thick, semi-solid consistency. Remove from heat and tip into a bowl, then leave to cool for a few minutes. Beat in the eggs, one at a time, with a spatula or wooden spoon until fully incorporated. Transfer to a piping bag.

Heat the oven to 180°C fan (400°F). Line a baking sheet with greaseproof paper, cut the tip of the piping bag to a width of about 2.5 cm (1 in), then pipe the chouxs straight down into blobs about 5 cm (2 in) in diameter – you will get 6 blobs out of the full batch. Top with sprinkles or pearl sugar, then bake for 25 minutes until fully inflated and golden brown. Remove from the oven and leave to cool.

To assemble, whip the cream, sugar and vanilla together until firm peaks form, then transfer to a piping bag. Cut the choux buns open on one side, like clamshells, then pipe some melon custard into their bases. Pipe the whipped cream on top, overflowing out of the choux, then pack a handful of chopped melon onto the surface of the cream. Keep in the refrigerator until ready to serve. Eat them as fresh as possible.

MILK PURIN
PURIN プリン

One of Japan's favourite little desserts is *purin*, a steamed, set caramel custard similar to a flan. In Hokkaido, these often showcase the quality of local milk and cream, but there are many variations as well. I have included one infused with lavender and honey inspired by the version they sell at Farm Tomita (page 193) here. The base recipe is adapted from one by Sakie Nakajima.[63]

MAKES 8 LITTLE PURIN

CARAMEL
70 g (2½ oz/scant ⅓ cup) caster (superfine) or granulated sugar
1 tbsp plus ½ tbsp water

CUSTARD
330 ml (11¼ fl oz/1⅓ cups) whole milk
150 ml (5 fl oz/scant ⅔ cup) double (heavy) cream
1 tsp vanilla extract or paste
1 whole egg
3 egg yolks
⅛ tsp cornflour (cornstarch)
80 g (2¾ oz/⅓ cup) golden caster (superfine) sugar

METHOD
To make the caramel, combine the sugar and 1 tbsp water in a saucepan and set over a medium heat. Melt without stirring, then let the sugar caramelise to a deep, dark brown. Remove from the heat and add the ½ tbsp water, swirling the pan to combine. Divide the caramel equally into 8 little glass pots or ramekins – about ½ tbsp caramel per pot.

To make the custard, combine the milk, cream and vanilla in a saucepan and bring to the boil, then remove from the heat. In a mixing bowl, beat together the egg, yolks, cornflour and sugar. Pour a splash of the milk and cream into the egg mixture and whisk well, then slowly pour in the remaining milk and cream, whisking as you go.

Heat the oven to 140°C fan (300°F). Pass the custard through a sieve and into a jug. Pour the mix into the pots, then place them in a baking tin (pan). Heat some water to about 80°C (176°F) (steaming, but below simmering), and pour this into the tray, to a depth of about half that of the custard in the pots. Cover the whole tray with foil, sealing the edges well, then bake for 35–40 minutes until the custards have set but are still wobbly. Remove the puddings from the tray and dry them on a cloth, then transfer to the refrigerator to set. Serve chilled.

LAVENDER HONEY PURIN VARIATION

Replace the sugar in the custard with the same weight of honey (you don't have to use lavender honey but it's nice to commit to a theme). Add 1 tsp lavender buds, lightly crushed, to the milk and cream as you heat it. If you like, you can also add purple food colouring.

お　　　土　　　産

10,000 REASONS
TO BUY THE OMIYAGE

*To try something I didn't have a chance to try while I was actually here •
To boast: look where I've been! • Because it really is something special, and
so are you, so I want you to have it • Because the packaging is just so pretty •
Because when I get home I'll need something to cheer myself up • Because
when I get home there will be someone asking me what I brought them •
Because this has been one of my favourite places in the world, and I want
a memento of this experience • Because this is one of my favourite places
in the world, and I buy it every time I visit, like a ritual • To say I love you •
To say I missed you • To say I really wish you could have been here • To say
I'm sorry I left you behind • To say I hope you can come here someday, too. •
To say thank you for being who you are • To say thank you for meeting with
me – it might have been just a professional obligation to you, but it meant a lot
to me • Because I have a professional obligation • Because I have a cultural
obligation • Because everyone else is buying the omiyage and I've got FOMO
• To say I know you've been homesick, and I hope this will help, if only a little •
To support a local business (that's local to someone else) • Because chocolate
oovorod potato chips?! Oh hell yes • Because it was so good the first time, and
I must have it again • Because I need it as a reference for when I try to recreate
it at home • Because the ingredients from this area really are excellent •
Because this town has nothing else to offer • Because it's fun and
exciting – not just the omiyage itself, but the act of buying it •
Because I may never be back here again.*

I had intended to include more recipes recreating some of Hokkaido's most
iconic omiyage, only to find that even the seemingly simplest ones were
nearly impossible to make at home. This included the famous Shiroi Koibito:
fine, sandy biscuits sandwiching a thin layer of chocolate. Turns out that to
make these well, you need both a hard-to-find silicone baking mould and
several years' experience working in a Parisian pâtisserie. You're actually
better off just going to Hokkaido and buying them. And I am okay with that.
It's part of what makes them special.

However, there are a few classic Hokkaido confections which are actually
relatively easy to make. Two of them – refreshing Yūbari cantaloupe jelly
and crunchy chocolate-covered corn – are made by Hori, a confectioner
based in Sunagawa. Then there's the world-famous chocolate-covered
potato chips, produced by the Sapporo chocolatier Royce'. If you're a
sweet-and-salty kind of person, you may want to double or triple the recipe
for these.

MELON JELLY

MERON ZERİ メロンゼリー

MAKES 4 JELLIES

400 g (14 oz) very ripe, very sweet cantaloupe melon
   (prepared weight)
2 tbsp white wine
1–6 tbsp caster (superfine) sugar (as needed)
1 tsp agar flakes
melon essence, as needed

METHOD

Blend the cantaloupe to a purée in a blender along with
the wine, then give it a taste. If it is quite sweet, add just
a tablespoonful of sugar; if it is not so sweet, add more.
The purée may foam up when blended; if so, let the foam
dissipate before proceeding with the recipe.

   Transfer half of the purée to a pan, then stir in the
agar flakes and let them bloom for 30 minutes. Bring
the mixture to the boil, then cook for 5 minutes, stirring
occasionally, until the agar dissolves completely, then
remove from the heat. Combine with the remaining melon
purée and taste the mixture. If it is insufficiently melony,
add a few drops of melon essence and stir well. Pass
the liquid through a fine sieve, then pour into little pots –
ideally plastic, so that they can be squeezed to loosen
the jellies when they are tipped out. Chill in the refrigerator
until completely set, and enjoy very cold.

CRISPY SWEETCORN CHOCOLATE

TŌKIBI CHOKO とうきびチョコ

MAKES 6 LITTLE BARS

100 g (3½ oz) white or milk chocolate, roughly chopped
40 g (1½ oz) toasted corn/'corn nuts' (ideally unsalted
    or lightly salted), coarsely chopped
20 g (¾ oz) hazelnuts, toasted and coarsely chopped

METHOD

Melt the chocolate in either a bain marie or the
microwave, then stir in the remaining ingredients.
If you have suitable moulds, spoon the mixture into
them to make little bars; if not, the chocolate can be set
as a single slab, then cut into portions with a sharp knife.
Keep the chocolate in the refrigerator until set, but
enjoy at room temperature.

POTATO CHIP CHOCOLATE

POTETO CHIPPU CHOKORĒTO ポテトチップチョコレート

MAKES ABOUT 2-4 SERVINGS

30 g (1 oz) salted, ridge-cut crisps (chips)
100 g (3½ oz) chocolate (any kind, but I prefer milk)

METHOD

The crisps for this need to be relatively large and intact:
30 g (1 oz) was the yield I got from a 45 g (1½ oz) bag,
so buy about 50% more than you'll actually need.
Melt the chocolate in a microwave or bain marie, then
dip one side of each crisp into the chocolate and lay out
in a single layer on a baking paper-lined tray. Set in the
refrigerator, then transfer to an airtight container and
keep at room temperature. They stay crunchy for
about a week.

'SNOWMELT' CHEESECAKE
HOMAGE TO SHINYA

SHINYA NO OMĀJU NO YUKIDOKI CHĪZUKĒKI 新谷のオマージュの雪どけチーズケーキ

This iconic cheesecake, made by Furano's Shinya bakery, gets its name from its whipped cream topping, which is thwacked with the back of a spoon to create little snowdrift-like peaks. It comes in many flavours. But I like the original best; it has two crusts and three layers, which keeps things interesting, and the light, melt-in-your-mouth texture is a beautiful carrier for the strong, buttery cheese flavour of the filling. You will need two 15 cm (6 in) fluted tart tins (pans) for this, with a depth of 3–4 cm (1–1½ in).

MAKES 2 × 15 CM (6 IN) CHEESECAKES - 12 LITTLE SLICES IN TOTAL

PÂTE SUCRÉE CRUST
120 g (4¼ oz/1 cup) plain (all-purpose) flour
50 g (1¾ oz/scant ½ cup) icing (powdered) sugar, sifted
40 g (1½ oz) salted butter, at room temperature and cubed
1 medium egg

PECAN BISCUIT BASE
45 g (1½ oz) digestive biscuits (graham crackers)
60 g (2 oz/⅔ cup) pecans
40 g (1½ oz) salted butter, melted
⅛ tsp ground cinnamon

FILLING
4 egg yolks
95 g (3⅓ oz/½ cup) golden caster (superfine) sugar
¾ tsp cornflour (cornstarch)
⅛ tsp lemon juice
⅛ tsp almond extract
2½ tbsp whipping cream
2½ tbsp milk
1 slice of American cheese
15 g (½ oz) margarine
4 g (⅛ oz) powdered gelatine
375 g (13¼ oz) cream cheese

TO ASSEMBLE AND COOK
70 g (2½ oz) smooth, tart berry jam
    reserved pâte sucrée
plain (all-purpose) flour, for dusting
reserved pecan biscuit crumb
reserved cheese filling
150 ml (5 fl oz/scant ⅔ cup) whipping cream
2 tbsp icing (powdered) sugar
¼ tsp vanilla extract

METHOD

Start by making the crust. Use a food processor or a pastry cutter to mix together the flour, sugar and butter until it forms a coarse, sandy texture. Stir in the egg and mix well. Wrap in cling film (plastic wrap) and rest in the refrigerator for 1–2 hours.

Next, combine all the pecan biscuit base ingredients in a food processor and blend to a coarse crumb.

Then make the filling by whisking together the egg yolks, sugar, cornflour, lemon juice and almond extract in a mixing bowl until smooth. Combine the cream, milk, cheese slice and margarine in a small saucepan and bring to a low boil, then switch off the heat and whisk in the gelatine. Leave to cool slightly, whisking a few more times to melt the cheese and dissolve the gelatine.

Slowly pour the milk mixture into the egg mixture while whisking constantly. Finally, whisk in the cream cheese until smooth.

Preheat the oven to 180°C fan (400°F). Roll out the pâte sucrée into a rectangle about 45 cm (18 in) long and 7 cm (3 in) wide, with a thickness of about 3 mm (⅛ in). Cut the rectangle into four strips, about 22.5 cm (9 in) by 3.5 cm (1½ in) each, and use these to line the edges of each tart tin (pan), pressing firmly into the grooves to secure it in place. Divide the pecan biscuit crumb into the bottom of each tart tin, and pack it down firmly using the back of a spoon, to form a solid, dense crust. Transfer to the oven and blind bake for 15 minutes. Remove the crusts and leave to cool before proceeding.

Once the crusts are cool, trim any excess pastry from around the rim of the tart tin with a sharp knife. Divide the jam between each tin, in the centre of the biscuit bases, then use the back of a spoon to gently spread it out in a thin layer covering the base. Divide the cheese filling evenly into each jam-lined crust, using a palette knife to smooth and flatten the filling's surface. Place back in the oven and cook for 25 minutes. If your oven does not distribute heat evenly, rotate the cheesecakes halfway through. Remove from the oven and leave to cool, then transfer to the refrigerator to chill completely.

Whip the cream, sugar and vanilla together until soft peaks form. Transfer the whipped cream to a piping bag, then pipe it onto the surface of each cheesecake. Use the back of a spoon to gently whack the surface of the cream to form irregular snowdrift-like peaks. This can be served immediately, or kept in the refrigerator for up to two days. It can also be frozen.

LAMINATED MILK BREAD

MIRU FĪYU SHOKUPAN ミルフィーユ食パン

I didn't want to include a milk bread recipe. Here's the thing: Hokkaido milk bread is bread made with Hokkaido milk, not a particular style of bread from Hokkaido. Milk bread made outside of Hokkaido, without Hokkaido milk, is not Hokkaido milk bread.

Having said all of that: who am I to deny my readers such a delicious bake? Of course, there are already a *lot* of milk bread recipes out there, so I thought I'd try something different. This is a laminated milk bread, inspired by one I bought at Heart Bread Antique in Sapporo. It is essentially a cross between milk bread and a croissant, and is every bit as delicious as that sounds.

Don't want a laminated milk bread? Well what's wrong with you?!? Just kidding – go ahead and make the bread without the lamination, it will still work. This recipe is informed by Matt Adlard's tropézienne cube from *Bake it Better*.

MAKES ONE 30 CM (11¾ IN) LOAF – ENOUGH FOR ABOUT 15-20 SLICES

MILK ROUX
150 g (5½ oz) whole milk
75 g (2½ oz/generous ½ cup) plain (all-purpose) flour

DOUGH
225 g (8 oz) whole milk
2 eggs
14 g (½ oz) dried yeast
620 g (1 lb 5¾ oz/5 cups) plain (all-purpose) flour
10 g (⅓ oz) salt
50 g (1¾ oz) honey
25 g (1 oz/¼ cup) caster (superfine) sugar
50 g (1¾ oz) butter, diced, at room temperature

LAMINATING AND BAKING
250 g (9 oz) butter
2 tbsp double (heavy) cream

METHOD

To make the roux, stir together the milk and flour in a medium microwave-safe bowl and microwave for 2 minutes (800W), stirring well every 30 seconds. Leave to cool to body temperature or lower before proceeding with the recipe.

For the dough, combine the milk, eggs and yeast in the bowl of a stand mixer fitted with the dough hook, and mix on medium speed for a minute or two, until the eggs are beaten. Add the flour, salt, honey and sugar. Switch the mixer on to low speed, then tear the roux into little chunks and drop them into the mixer, one by one, then add the butter as well. Switch the speed up to medium-low (speed 2 on my KitchenAid, for reference), and knead for 10–15 minutes.

At this point, check that your dough passes the 'windowpane test'. You should be able to grab a blob of dough and stretch it out to a thinness that allows you to see through it. If the dough tears, or stretches into strings rather than sheets, keep kneading. Once your dough has passed this test, tip it out onto a tray, cover loosely with cling film, and place in the fridge for six hours (or overnight) to rest.

To make the butter block, take the butter out of the fridge about an hour before you intend to start the lamination process. Cut the butter into slices about 5 mm (¼ in) thick, then arrange the slices on a sheet of baking parchment, in a rectangle measuring 15 × 25 cm (6 × 10 in). Place another sheet of baking parchment on top of the butter, then roll across the surface with a rolling pin, to press together the gaps in the butter and make a solid rectangle.

Lightly flour the countertop, then roll the dough out into a rectangle about 33 × 27 cm (13 × 10 in). Place the butter block onto one half of the rectangle of dough, and fold over the other half, like a book, enclosing the butter. At this point, the butter should be just warm enough to be pliable, but if your kitchen is particularly cold, you might need to let it rest before proceeding. If at any point, you feel or see the butter cracking as you fold the dough, pause for 15 minutes or so, then come back and try again.

Roll the dough out once again into a large rectangle, 33 × 27 cm (13 × 10 in). Fold in half again (like a book), then into thirds again (like a letter). You now have 6 layers of butter. Rest the dough for 15 mintues to let the gluten relax, then repeat this process (roll – book fold – letter fold) once more. At the end of the process you will have 36 layers of butter.

Grease the inside of a 12 or 13 cm (4¾–5 in) square Pullman loaf tin (pan) with the double cream, including the inside of the tin's lid. Roll your dough out to a large square the same length as the tin (for me this is 30 cm (11¾ in)), then roll the dough up like a carpet, and transfer to the tin, with the spiral edges facing outwards towards either end. Leave to prove until the dough has risen to within 1–2 cm (½–¾ in) of the top of the tin – I find this is best done overnight in the fridge.

Preheat the oven to 170ºC fan (375°F), then slide the lid onto the tin, and bake for 1 hour 15 minutes. Remove the bread from the tin as soon as it is done, and leave to cool on a wire rack.

The bread is fantastic as is but benefits from toasting, and a drizzle of condensed milk or a thin spread of jam. It will keep for about five days, but even when it does go stale, it will still be delicious once toasted.

MELON PAN VARIATION

Half a batch of this bread dough, without the lamination, will yield eight melon pan. Simply form the dough into big balls then top each one with a round of cookie dough (100 g/3½ oz salted butter, 70 g/2½ oz/scant ⅓ cup caster (superfine) sugar, 30 g/1 oz light brown sugar, 1 egg, 1 tsp vanilla extract, a few drops of melon essence, 240 g/8½ oz/2 cups plain (all-purpose) flour and ½ tsp baking powder). Prove until poofy, and bake for 18 minutes at 170ºC fan (375°F). If you like, you can fill the finished pan with melon custard (see recipe, page 201).

KUSHIRO

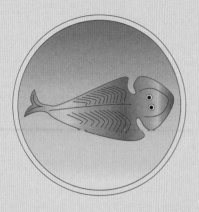

釧
路

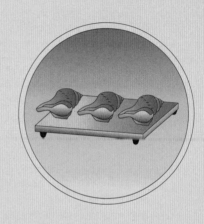

TSURUMARU

MASCOT: TSURUMARU

Tsurumaru, officially the 'Main Character of the Mizu-no-Kamuy Tourism Area,' a red-crowned crane who is eternally five years old. He carries a marimo on a strap over his shoulder and is referred to as an *amaenbō* – a sweet mama's boy.

POPULATION: 157,826

ETYMOLOGY

Several theories from Ainu exist, including *kus ru* (crossroads), *kus sir* (mountains facing a river), or possibly a shared etymology with Kussharo, *kutcaro* – meaning 'throat' and referring to the point where Lake Kussharo drains into the Kushiro River.

KUSHIRO 釧路 釧路 釧路

In London we don't have to deal with snow regularly enough for us to think of it as something to be dealt with. Even on the very rare occasion when snow causes problems, it's fun and exciting because it's so out of the ordinary. Not so in Hokkaido (or Wisconsin, where I'm from). Of course it has its moments, when it blankets the earth with quietude. But then it gets real. Then it gets ugly. It gets driven over, trod on, ploughed aside, blackened by all of the exhaust in the air and the crud on the ground.

Kushiro brings all of this home: snow here is just a fact of urban life, not some winter wonderland. Like a lot of mid-sized cities in Japan, Kushiro's population is both shrinking and ageing, and it feels a little forlorn. It gets more lively at night, when the city's many excellent izakaya and robata joints fill up with locals washing down whelks and whale with highballs and hot sake. But when you pay your tab and head back out, you find Kushiro even quieter than it was before, muffled by the snow.

The morning after a blizzard, my contact, Ōno-san, and I have a hearty kattedon (seafood rice bowl) breakfast (page 184) and drive up to Lake Akan. Along the way, we stop at the International Crane Centre, a conservatory and museum dedicated to the repopulation of tanchō, the red-crowned cranes with great symbolic significance. This wasn't on my itinerary, as the cranes have nothing to do with food. So thank God for Ōno-san, who suggested the detour.

The colonisation of Hokkaido resulted in devastating habitat loss for the red-crowned cranes, particularly in the Kushiro wetlands. Their population plummeted to only 40 individuals in the 1960s, when conservation efforts began. Thanks in part to the Crane Centre, they've made a spectacular recovery; there are now almost 2,000 of them. And they are a joy to see. They are surprisingly humongous, alternately majestic and awkward as they dance and peck and swoop and call.

They could have been lost forever. But the people of Kushiro saw this happening, and intervened. I love stories like this. They restore my faith in humanity.

We stop a little further down the road for a mid-morning ice cream. I get fresh milk flavour, in a maple sugar cone. It tastes like the snow-covered farmland all around us. It tastes like Hokkaido.

KUSHIRO 釧路 釧路 釧路

MELON SODA FLOAT

MERON SŌDA FURŌTO メロンソーダフロート

You hardly need a recipe for this. But I'm including one anyway, for a few reasons. One is that it is perhaps the simplest and most direct way to enjoy the milk-melon flavour combination that is so popular in Hokkaido. Another is so that I can include a gorgeous studio photo of it, because it is so visually striking – bright white against fluorescent Kerry green. And about that green colour: weirdly, some of the Japanese melon soda available these days is no longer green, but clear. So this means you have to add the green colour yourself, with food dye. And you *do* have to add it – it's just not the same without it.

chilled melon soda, or melon syrup mixed with soda water, as needed
green food colouring, as needed (optional)
ice cream, as needed
maraschino cherries, as needed (optional)

METHOD

If your melon soda is colourless, add enough green food colouring to make you squint when you look at it. Pour into glasses and top with one or two scoops of ice cream. Garnish with a cherry (if you like) and serve with a spoon and a straw.

'DOUBLE FROMAGE' CHEESECAKE
HOMAGE TO LE TAO

LE TAO NO HOMĀJU NO 'DŪBURU FUROMĀJU' CHĪZUKĒKI ルタオのオマージュの「ドゥーブルフロマージュ」チーズケーキ

Hokkaido is a land of many cheesecakes, but perhaps the most famous of them all, the one that's graduated from the omiyage stands of Chitose to the big leagues of Narita and Haneda, is the 'double fromage' from Otaru's Le Tao. This double-layered cheesecake is like eating a cloud made of cheese. Even the crust is light and delicate, made of cake rather than biscuits or pastry. It is a symphony of softness, and it is surprisingly easy to make. This recipe is based on versions from *Macaroni*[64] and *HidaMari Cooking*.[65]

SERVES 6

CRUMB
butter, as needed, for greasing
about 200 g (7 oz) sponge cake
100 ml (3½ fl oz/scant ½ cup) double (heavy) cream
1 tbsp icing (powdered) sugar

BAKED LAYER
100 g (3½ oz) cream cheese
50 g (1¾ oz) mascarpone
50 g (1¾ oz/¼ cup) golden caster (superfine) sugar
50 ml (1¾ fl oz/3½ tbsp) double (heavy) cream
1 egg
1½ tsp cornflour (cornstarch)
⅛ tsp salt

SET LAYER
1 tbsp water
1 tbsp milk
1 tsp powdered gelatine
30 g (1 oz) golden caster (superfine) sugar
150 g (5½ oz) mascarpone
100 ml (3½ fl oz/scant ½ cup) double (heavy) cream
¼ tsp vanilla extract (optional)

METHOD
This recipe works best if everything is at room temperature.

Line a 15 cm (6 in) cake tin (pan) (springform, or with a removable base) neatly with baking parchment. Lightly grease the paper with butter. Trim the crusts off the sponge cake and cut the rest of it into chunks, then place in a food processor. Blitz to a fluffy crumb. Pack about a quarter of the crumbs into the bottom of the cake tin, pressing down gently to form an even layer. Preheat the oven to 150°C fan (325°F).

To make the baked layer, smash the cheeses and the sugar together until well mixed, then stir in all of the remaining ingredients and mix until smooth. I recommend using a spatula rather than a whisk for this, so you don't incorporate too much air into the mix. Pour the mixture into the prepared cake tin, even out the surface with an offset spatula, then bake for 20 minutes. Remove from the oven and leave to cool.

Stir together the water, milk and gelatine in a small dish and leave to soften for at least 10 minutes. Heat the liquid until warm (not boiling) in the microwave – this should take only 10 seconds or so. Stir to fully dissolve the gelatine. Combine the gelatine liquid with the sugar and stir until it dissolves, then whisk together with all of the remaining ingredients until the mixture is visibly more airy. Pour this mixture onto the cooled baked layer, then transfer to the refrigerator to chill.

To finish, whip the cream and sugar together until very soft peaks form – the cream should still be pourable. Remove the cheesecake from the tin, then place it on a cake stand or up-turned bowl so the sides are fully accessible. Spread the whipped cream in a very thin layer all over the surface of the cake, then use your hands to gently press the rest of the cake crumb into the cream, fully coating the cake. Keep in the refrigerator until ready to serve.

FUNDAMENTAL

料理の基本

& RESOURCES

推奨読書

WAKKANAI

稚内

DASHINOSUKE

© Wakkanai Tourism Association

MASCOT
Dashinosuke, a seal who came to Wakkanai for the delicious seafood. His greenish colour and kelp-like flippers are a consequence of eating too much kombu.

ETYMOLOGY
From the Ainu *yam wakka nay*, 'cold drinking water river'.

POPULATION: 31,195

稚内 **W A K K A N A I** 稚内

THE END.

Cape Sōya, Wakkanai: the northernmost point in Japan.
You can go no further. You can stand here, and gaze across the Sea of Okhotsk, and if you're lucky you can see Russia. There's a satisfying feeling of finality. Take a selfie, take a deep breath, pat yourself on the back and buy yourself a commemorative refrigerator magnet. You made it to the end!
... And then what?

Then you turn your back to the sea and you face Wakkanai, Hokkaido, the entire nation of Japan, stretching out forever into the distance before you. That feeling of closure vanishes, replaced by a recognition that you haven't even scratched the surface. There is no end. You can never tie a little bow on it and put it up on a shelf, because you *haven't done a goddamn thing*.

Look far and wide; then look close. Marvel at the sheer size of it all, then marvel even more at the details within that expanse. *My God, it's full of stars.*

Reaching the northernmost point of Japan was a dream of mine. I'm not sure why. For bragging rights, maybe – just to say I'd been there. But I was surprised at how it really did feel like an accomplishment, at least for a minute or two.

But there's work to do. More places to go, more things to see and food to try. I buy my magnet, get back into the van, nod goodbye to Sakhalin, and we drive up into the hills. We turn onto the Shiroi Michi, a former construction access road which has now been paved with billions of scallop shells, brilliant white in the September sun.

We visit a fishmonger, Uroko-Tei, where they are processing various types of fish; to be sold, somewhat sneakily, in places that are more famous for those fish: fugu to Shimonoseki, whole dried cod to Kansai, their roe to Fukuoka, their gills to Ōita. At a local grocery store, Aizawa, my guide, Mia, recommends the local milk, so I buy a bottle to have later. I don't even like milk. But I just know it'll be good.

At first, Wakkanai feels pretty much like any other similar-sized town in Hokkaido, but then you notice that the signs on the shopfronts along Wakkanai's main shopping street are displayed in Russian – a relic of a time when relations between the two countries were a little warmer. Not too long ago, there was regular boat traffic between Wakkanai and Sakhalin, for both trade and tourism, but not anymore. The city feels a little quieter than it probably should, but it still sees a fair amount of visitors, excitedly taking photos as they disembark at Wakkanai Station, where distance markers tell you how far you are from Tokyo (1,549.7 km, if you're curious).

稚内 **W A K K A N A I** 稚内

→

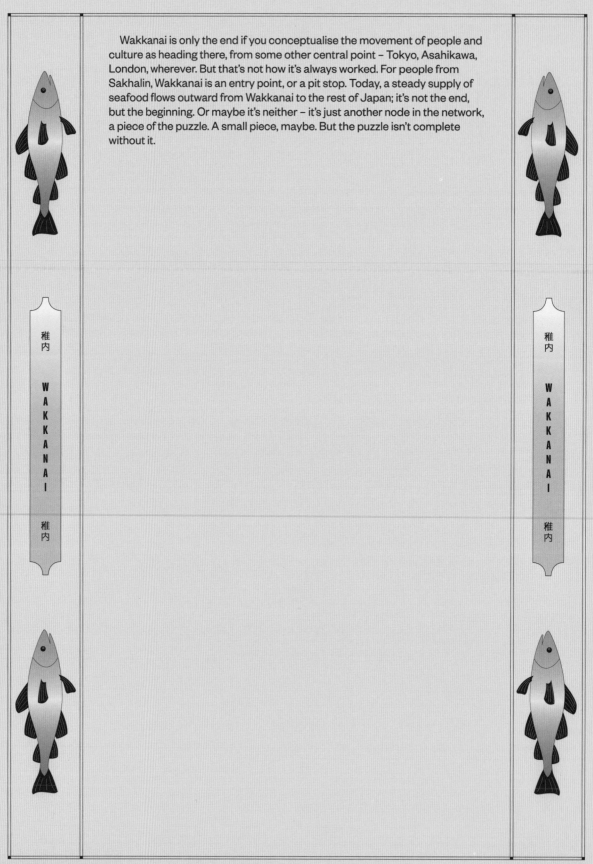

Wakkanai is only the end if you conceptualise the movement of people and culture as heading there, from some other central point – Tokyo, Asahikawa, London, wherever. But that's not how it's always worked. For people from Sakhalin, Wakkanai is an entry point, or a pit stop. Today, a steady supply of seafood flows outward from Wakkanai to the rest of Japan; it's not the end, but the beginning. Or maybe it's neither – it's just another node in the network, a piece of the puzzle. A small piece, maybe. But the puzzle isn't complete without it.

稚内

WAKKANAI

稚内

稚内

WAKKANAI

稚内

RAMEN BROTH, THREE WAYS

CHINTAN, DŌBUTSU-KEI, NIBAN NO RĀMEN SŪPU 清湯・動物系・二番のラーメンスープ

This recipe can be made in three different ways to make three very different broths, starting with the same ingredients. One is a light, clear *chintan* suitable for shio ramen (page 155) and, with slight modification, for Kushiro ramen (page 164). The other is an 'animal style' (*dōbutsu-kei*) broth, also a chintan but one which is heavier and cloudier, with more dissolved fat and collagen from a more vigorous boil. It is suitable for Sapporo Miso Ramen (page 152), Curry Ramen (pages 166–167) and offal ramen (page 163). As is typical of most Hokkaido ramen, this recipe contains more pork than chicken, but feel free to change this ratio as you like. I have also included a method for a cloudy *niban* ('number two') broth, which does not feature in any recipes but can be made as a general-purpose utility broth if you want to make the most out of your bones.

MAKES 2.5 LITRES (84½ FL OZ/10½ CUPS) OF DŌBUTSU-KEI OR 3.5 LITRES (118 FL OZ/14¾ CUPS) OF CHINTAN

750 g (1 lb 10 oz) pork ribs
500 g (1 lb 2 oz) pork neck or back bones
500 g (1 lb 2 oz) chicken frames (this is roughly
    equivalent to the carcass of 1 large chicken)
250 g (9 oz) chicken wings
1 onion, quartered, unpeeled (optional)
1 garlic bulb, halved (optional)
50 g (1¾ oz) fresh ginger root,
    washed and thinly sliced (optional)

METHOD

For either broth, place all of the bones (but not the vegetables) in a large stockpot (at least 8 litre (270½ fl oz/33¾ cup) capacity) and cover with water. Bring to a low boil over a high heat. As the water boils, skim off the scum that forms on the surface. You will have to do this repeatedly for the first half hour or so of the boil to ensure the broth doesn't develop a muddy flavour and grey appearance.

FOR CHINTAN BROTH

Once the scum formation has subsided, reduce the heat to very low, and place a lid on the pan. The broth should be held at around 85°C (185°F), so use a thermometer if you have one – if you don't, the broth should be just steaming, with a few small bubbles rising to the surface every now and then. Maintain this temperature for 5 hours. If you are having trouble keeping it at this temperature on the hob, consider cooking the broth in the oven, set to 120–140°C (275–300°F). After 5 hours, add the vegetables, if using, and continue to cook for another hour. Remove the bones from the pot, then pass the broth through a sieve. Measure the liquid; it should be about 3.5 litres (118 fl oz/14¾ cups), so if it is significantly more or less than this, either reduce or top up with water to achieve the correct amount.

FOR DŌBUTSU-KEI BROTH

Once the scum has subsided, keep the heat at medium-high and place a lid on the pan. The broth should be kept at a steady, low boil – bubbling away, but not too aggressively. You will have to top up the water periodically to maintain the level. Keep boiling for 5 hours, then add the vegetables, if using, and continue to cook for another hour. Remove the bones from the pot, then pass the broth through a sieve. Measure the liquid; it should be about 2.5 litres (84½ fl oz/10½ cups), so if it is significantly more or less than this, either reduce or top up with water to achieve the correct amount.

FOR NIBAN BROTH

Take the leftover bones from either broth and place them in a pot and cover with water. Boil hard for 3–4 hours; replenish the aromatic vegetables in the final hour if you want a fresher flavour. Remove the bones from the pot and pass the broth through a sieve. All broths should be cooled rapidly and then transferred to the refrigerator, where they will keep for about a week.

SHŌYU TARE

SHŌYU TARE
醤油タレ

This is a simple but well-rounded shōyu tare, based on *kaeshi* seasoning used for soba, good for both Asahikawa- and Kushiro- style ramen.

**MAKES 345 ML (11²/₃ FL OZ/1¹/₂ CUPS),
ENOUGH FOR ABOUT 6-10 BOWLS OF RAMEN**

100 ml (3½ fl oz/scant ½ cup) marudaizu shōyu
100 ml (3½ fl oz/scant ½ cup) nama (unpasteurised) shōyu
100 ml (3½ fl oz/scant ½ cup) usukuchi shōyu
3 tbsp hon-mirin
1 tsp Demerara sugar

METHOD

Stir together all ingredients until the sugar dissolves. Use 30–60 ml (2–4 tbsp) per 300 ml (10 fl oz/1¼ cups) of broth, depending on your taste.

BASIC CHĀSHŪ METHOD

KIHONTEKI NA CHĀSHŪ NO TSUKURIKATA
基本的なチャーシューの作り方

There are countless ways to make chāshū, but most Hokkaido ramen tend to keep it pretty old school, *nikomi* style, by simply boiling it and then soaking it in a tare, such as the Shōyu Tare, opposite, and Pork Tare on page 243. Typically, the meat is boiled in broth, but of course this will change the broth's consistency and appearance, so it's best not to cook it in a chintan (page 229) destined for Hakodate or Kushiro ramen, where clarity is key. The meat should be parboiled for 5–10 minutes in water and then rinsed clean before starting the main boil, in order to remove the blood from the meat.

METHOD

About 80–100 g (2¾–3½ oz) of meat (raw weight) will be plenty for each bowl. Loin, belly and shoulder (all with the rind removed) are all common in Hokkaido ramen, and how long you boil them varies by cut, but also by personal preference. Here is a general guide, per 500 g (1 lb 2 oz) of meat.

LOIN: 20–25 minutes
SHOULDER: 45 minutes–1 hour
BELLY (ROLLED): 1 hour–1 hour 15 minutes

Again, these timings will vary depending on a lot of factors, so use your best judgement for doneness. Once cooked, transfer to a container with about 1 tbsp tare per 100 g (3½ oz) of meat; I usually use a plastic bag for this, which helps maintain even coverage. Chill in the refrigerator, then slice thinly. I re-warm chāshū in the oven, but it can also be grilled (broiled) or blowtorched.

ラ ー メ ン の 王 国

RAMEN NOODLE MAKING METHOD

MEN NO UCHIKATA 麺の打ち方

Though all of the noodle recipes here are a little different, they are all made the same way:

1. Stir the measured kansui (alkaline minerals, potassium carbonate and sodium carbonate) and salt into the measured water, until they dissolve. If the recipe calls for it, stir riboflavin to the water as well.

2. Measure the flours and other dry ingredients (such as powdered egg) into a mixing bowl and mix well.

3. Slowly pour the water into the flour, mixing as you go, to hydrate the flour evenly – a stand mixer is useful for this.

4. Compress the dough into a solid mass, and rest it for an hour in a plastic bag or container.

5. Cut the dough into four pieces and roll them out to a maximum thickness of 1 cm (½ in).

6. Roll the dough out using a pasta roller (ideally electric) to form cohesive sheets, then decrease the thickness of the roller incrementally until the desired thickness is achieved.

7. Cover the dough and rest for another hour. Trim the edges, and cut using the required attachment.

Making noodles is a tricky, technical process that I do not have space to explain fully here. For in-depth instructions, seek out Ramen Lord's *Book of Ramen* (a free eBook), Hugh Amano and Sarah Becan's *Let's Make Ramen* or my own *Ramen Forever*. Most of the following recipes are based on ones found in Ryōichi Nishio's *Ramen Taizen* ('*The Complete Ramen*'). All of these recipe make four portions.

HAKODATE-STYLE NOODLES

HAKODATE RÂMEN NO MEN 函館ラーメンの麺

Hakodate soups are very light, so the noodles should readily absorb the broth in order to carry its flavour. Kansui, protein and hydration levels are moderate, to keep the dough from becoming tough.

MAKES 4 PORTIONS
145 ml water
4 g salt
4 g kansui
a pinch of riboflavin (optional)
380 g strong white bread flour
20 g plain (all-purpose) flour
cornflour (cornstarch), for dusting

METHOD
Mix and roll as per the instructions on page 232. Cut to 2 × 2 mm. Dust with cornflour and either keep straight, or knead lightly to develop a curl. These can be cooked right away but they are better if you rest them for at least a day.

SAPPORO-STYLE NOODLES

SAPPORO RÂMEN NO MEN 札幌ラーメンの麺

Sapporo noodles are curly, chewy and distinctly yellow in colour. Their irregular form works perfectly with the full-bodied texture of miso ramen broth and its varied vegetable toppings, which also makes them great for Curry Ramen (page 167) and morumen (page 163). For a chewier structure, use a kansui blend with more sodium than potassium.

MAKES 4 PORTIONS
160 ml water
4 g salt
8 g kansui
⅛ tsp riboflavin
400 g strong white bread flour
8 g whole egg powder
12 g vital wheat gluten
cornflour (cornstarch), for dusting

METHOD
Mix and roll as per the instructions on page 232. Cut to 2 × 2 mm. Dust with cornflour and knead well to form a curl. Rest for at least a day, and up to a week, before cooking.

KUSHIRO-STYLE NOODLES

KUSHIRO RĀMEN NO MEN 釧路ラーメンの麺

Kushiro ramen noodles are unique in that they are very thin, but unlike most thin ramen noodles they are not hard and straight – they look and taste like a skinny version of Sapporo noodles. Ensure that these are aged at least two days, which will give them a denser texture that remains thin, rather than puffing up, upon boiling.

MAKES 4 PORTIONS
150 ml water
4 g salt
4 g kansui
a big pinch of riboflavin
360 g strong white bread flour
40 g plain (all-purpose) flour
5 g egg powder
cornflour (cornstarch), for dusting

METHOD
Mix and roll as per the instructions above. Cut to 1 × 1 mm. Dust with cornflour and knead well to form a curl. Rest for at least two days before cooking.

ASAHIKAWA-STYLE NOODLES

ASAHIKAWA RĀMEN NO MEN 旭川ラーメンの麺

Asahikawa noodles are very low hydration (less than 30%), which gives them a snappy yet tender texture, unusual among Hokkaido ramen. It is better to use a kansui blend that contains more potassium carbonate than sodium carbonate; Ramen Supply Co.'s Type III is ideal, as it also contains phosphates that assist in hydration. These are better if they are cooked on the softer side of al dente, so they become a little more absorbent.

Because there is so little water in this dough, it is *very* difficult to make. Prolonged resting (for several hours, or overnight) in between mixing and rolling, and again between rolling and cutting, will help the dough hydrate and relax. But if it's still not working, feel free to increase the water content up to 140 ml and the results will be similar.

MAKES 4 PORTIONS
125 ml water
4 g salt
6 g kansui
a pinch of riboflavin (optional)
320 g strong white bread flour
80 g plain (all-purpose) flour
10 g egg powder
cornflour (cornstarch), for dusting

METHOD
Mix and roll as per the instructions above. Cut to 1.5 × 1.5 mm. These can be kept straight or bunched up to develop a slight curl. Rest overnight before cooking.

RISHIRI

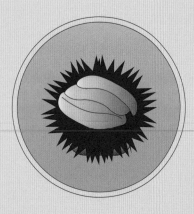

利尻

RISHIRIN

© Rishiri Town Development | Promotion Division, Commerce and Tourism Promotion Section

MASCOT
Rishirin, a length of Grade 3 Rishiri kombu, with an Ezo *kanzō* (day lily) blossom on her head, trousers in the shape of Mt Rishiri and two varieties of sea urchin on her back.

ETYMOLOGY
From the Ainu *ri sir*, 'high island'.

POPULATION: 4,085

People from Rishiri are tough. They have to be, because it's a tough place to live: a rocky island, dominated by the jagged peak of Mount Rishiri, a land of cold winds and heavy snow, frequently cut off from the rest of Japan by rough seas and stormy skies. In a way, it's no wonder the population of Rishiri is declining. Life on Rishiri is a challenge, and not everyone is up to it.

Which leaves the people who are, like Taketoshi Fujita, an 85-year-old kombu farmer, who also performs in a hip-hop group called Rishiri Boys who promote the island and its produce.[66] Or Casey Wahl and Javier Negrete, who have founded the microdistillery Kamui Whisky on the west coast of the island, inspired by its similarities to Islay. Or Takashi Ebina, one of the few representatives of a younger generation of fishermen dedicated to continuing the traditions of the island. On his website, Ebina-san writes, 'My father once told me that "life is just a way to kill time until you die." I want to live a life that will continue to challenge me, with all my strength, until I die.' Damn!

That's Rishiri people: tough. Not tough in the British sense that they've got a chip on their shoulder and they'll throw a bottle at you if you look at them funny, but in the sense that they remain resolute even in the face of harsh conditions. Thank God for people like this, because without them, there would be nobody to harvest the kombu: the best in Japan, and therefore, the world.

利尻

R
I
S
H
I
R
I

利尻

利尻

R
I
S
H
I
R
I

利尻

とろろ昆布

DASHI OF HOKKAIDO

A FIELD GUIDE

Dashi's spiritual home is Hokkaido: the land of kombu. Hokkaido is known for its premium kombu, and three of the most celebrated varieties – Rishiri, Hidaka and Rausu – all come from their namesake regions of the island. Rishiri is typically considered the best for dashi, with a strong aroma and high mineral content. (However, Rausu and Hidaka have a softer texture and are therefore better for eating.)[67] Try them all, and see which one best suits your own purposes.

While dashi is typically also flavoured with katsuobushi, other varieties of dried fish are common, as well. These include salmon, mackerel and shellfish such as squid and scallops. The following recipes explain how to use these to give your cooking a subtle Hokkaido accent.

KOMBU DASHI

KONBU DASHI 昆布出汁

MAKES 500 ML (17 FL OZ/GENEROUS 2 CUPS)

METHOD

Combine 600 ml (20 fl oz/2½ cups) water with
20 g (¾ oz) good-quality kombu. Leave to soak
overnight. Place over a low heat and bring to
80°C (176°F) (the barest of simmers – with just a few
bubbles breaking the surface of the water). Remove
from the heat and leave to cool to room temperature,
then remove the kombu. If using Hidaka kombu, this can
be further cooked and eaten in soups or as tsukudani.
If using Rishiri kombu, it can be soaked or simmered
in vinegar to soften, which will yield a kombu vinegar
(excellent for sushi rice or curing fish), and the kombu
can then be rinsed, cooked and eaten.

DRIED SCALLOP DASHI

HOSHI HOTATE DASHI 干し帆立出汁

MAKES 500 ML (17 FL OZ/GENEROUS 2 CUPS)

METHOD

Combine 600 ml (20 fl oz/2½ cups) water with
10–15 g (⅓–½ oz) dried scallops. Leave to soak overnight
then cook at a high simmer for 20 minutes. Remove
from the heat and leave to cool to room temperature.
Pass the dashi through a sieve. The boiled/rehydrated
scallops can be turned into tsukudani or chilli oil, or
simply folded through rice. This dashi can also be
infused with kombu for added umami and aroma. Simply
add 10–15 g (⅓–½ oz) of kombu along with the scallops
as they cold-infuse, but remove it just as the water
begins to simmer.

KEZURIBUSHI (DRIED FISH) DASHI

KEZURIBUSHI NO DASHI 削り節の出汁

MAKES 450 ML (15¼ FL OZ/SCANT 2 CUPS)

METHOD

Combine 600 ml (20 fl oz/2½ cups) water with 10 g (⅓ oz) kombu. Leave to soak for at least 4 hours; overnight is better. Place over a low heat and bring to 80°C (176°F). Add 15 g (½ oz) fushi (dried fish shavings) and sustain the simmer for 10 minutes, then remove from the heat and leave to cool to room temperature. Pass the dashi through a sieve, pressing down firmly on the solids with the back of a ladle to extract as much flavour as possible.

MEAT SAUCE

MĪTO SŌSU ミートソース

This sauce features in three recipes in this book: Spa-katsu (page 171), Sisco Rice (page 180) and the Lucky Pierrot Fatso Burger (page 126). It is based on a Mos Burger copycat recipe from *Delish Kitchen*.[68]

MAKES ABOUT 1.6 LITRES (54 FL OZ/6¾ CUPS)
50 g (1¾ oz) butter
2 tbsp lard
2 tbsp olive oil
3 small or 2 medium onions, finely chopped
2 stalks celery, finely chopped
4 carrots, finely chopped
6 garlic cloves, finely chopped
200 g (7 oz) minced (ground) pork
200 g (7 oz) minced (ground) beef
many grinds of black pepper
⅛ tsp freshly grated nutmeg
4 tbsp plain (all-purpose) flour
350 ml (12¼ fl oz/1½ cups) red wine
1 tin (400 g/14 oz) oxtail soup
2 beef stock cubes
400 g (14 oz) passata
100 g (3½ oz) tomato purée (paste)
2 tbsp shōyu
2 tbsp tonkatsu sauce
1 bay leaf (optional)
apple cider vinegar, sugar, salt and MSG, all to taste

METHOD

Melt the butter and lard together with the olive oil in a large casserole over a medium-high heat. Add the onions, celery, carrots and garlic and sauté for about 10 minutes until softened and lightly browned, then add the mince, pepper and nutmeg, break up the mince and continue to cook for another 8–10 minutes, stirring often, until the mince is cooked through and beginning to brown as well. Stir in the flour, ensuring there are no lumps, then stir in the wine and bring to the boil. Add the soup, stock cubes, passata, tomato purée, soy sauce, tonkatsu sauce and bay leaf (if using). Simmer for about 15 minutes, stirring often, until rich and thick, then adjust the flavour with apple cider vinegar, sugar, salt and MSG, to taste.

PORK TARE

YAKIBUTA NO TARE 焼き豚のタレ

This is a simple tare for grilled pork dishes, specifically Muroran Yakitori (page 98) and Obihiro Butadon (page 178), but it can be used on most meat and fatty fish. If you like, you can infuse it with aromatics such as garlic or ginger, or umami-rich ingredients like kombu or katsuobushi.

MAKES ABOUT 180 ML (6 FL OZ/³/₄ CUP)
6 tbsp shōyu
2 tbsp sake
2 tbsp Demerara or brown sugar
2 tbsp honey
2 tbsp mirin

METHOD
Combine all ingredients in a saucepan and bring to the boil. Boil for a couple minutes to dissolve the sugar and reduce very slightly. Leave to cool before using. Keep in the refrigerator.

RICE

GOHAN NO TAKIKATA ご飯の炊き方

METHOD
Allow 75–100 g (2½–3½ oz/⅓–scant ½ cup) rice per person. Measure the rice, then wash to remove excess starch and drain well. Place in a rice cooker or a saucepan along with 1.3 times (by weight) or 1.1 times (by volume) the amount of rice in water. (For example: for 300 g/360 ml (10½ oz/1½ cups) rice, use 390 g/396 ml (13¾ oz/1⅔ cups) water.) If using a rice cooker, cook according to the cooker's instructions. If using a saucepan, bring the rice to a boil over high heat, then place a lid on the pan and reduce the heat to very low. Steam for 15 minutes, then rest, off the heat, for 10 minutes before serving.

ENDNOTES AND
WORKS CITED

STATEMENT OF ATTRIBUTION

Culinary knowledge often comes to us in ways that are diffuse and indirect. In addition to the specific works listed below, the recipes and essays in this book have been informed by countless additional sources, everything from restaurant menus, blogs, Instagram accounts, individuals I met in Japan, TV shows and YouTube videos.

It is not possible to fully catalogue all of these sources, but I wish to expressly acknowledge and thank all of the unnamed people who have contributed to my understanding of Hokkaido food. In particular, I want to mention the individuals and institutions who have shared their knowledge of Ainu food, especially my interviewees on pages 17–27, Chef Hiroaki Kon, and the curatorial staff and educators at Upopoy, Pirka Kotan, Kushiro City Museum, and the Lake Akan Ainu Kotan.

I have cited specific sources both within the text and in the footnotes that follow, but there are a few I wanted to highlight in particular, as I found them so insightful and informative:

Golden Kamuy by Satoru Noda. The over-the-top violence in this manga makes it not to everyone's taste, but I know of no better resource in English when it comes to depictions of early modern Hokkaido food, especially Ainu cuisine.

Ainu Mosir, directed by Takeshi Fukunaga. I had intended to include a brief essay about this film, as I thought it was so good at expressing some of the key issues in Ainu society. It only obliquely touches on food, but is absolutely worth a watch.

The Spirit of Huci: Four Seasons of an Ainu Woman by Tomoko Keira. The only English-language Ainu cookbook I know of, full of recipes and practical information but also personal memories and cultural insights.

Hokkaido 150: Settler Colonialism and Indigeneity in Modern Japan and Beyond. This podcast series, produced by the University of British Columbia's Centre for Japanese Research, features historians and cultural scholars speaking on a wide range of subjects related to the Ainu and the colonisation of Hokkaido.

Shizen no Megumi – Ainu no Gohan 自然の恵み　アイヌのごはん by Hisakazu Fujimura and *Hokkaido Kyōdo Ryōri* 北海道郷土料理 by Sachiko Hoshizawa. These cookbooks, which were never out of reach as I did my research, focus on Ainu food and traditional Hokkaido regional cookery, respectively.

1   Brett L. Walker, *The Conquest of Ainu Lands: Ecology and Culture in Japanese Expansion*, 1590–1800 (University of California Press, 2001) 5–6.

2   Kumagai, K. 'Unilang • Ainu For Beginners,' Unilang, https://unilang.org/course.php?res=58

3   'アイヌモシリ', *Wikipedia: The Free Encyclopedia*, last edited 14 August 2024, https://ja.wikipedia.org/wiki/アイヌモシリ

4   Siripala, T. 2020, 'Far-right politics and indigenous Ainu activism in Japan', *Georgetown Journal of Asian Affairs*, vol. 6, pp. 36–44 http://hdl.handle.net/10822/1059391

5   Kotan no Kai, 'コタンの会とは？ABOUT', https://kotankai.jimdofree.com/コタンの会とは-about/

6   Yoshigaki, F. 2019, 'Ainu leaders bash bill for absence of their aboriginal rights', *The Asahi Shimbun*, March, https://www.asahi.com/ajw/articles/13066949

7   Upopoy National Museum and Park, 'Memorial Site', https://ainu-upopoy.jp/en/facility/cenotaph/

8   Odawara, N. 2020, '「"私はあなたの『アイヌ』ではない"」：小田原のどかが見た「ウポポイ（民族共生象徴空間）」', *Bijutsu Techō*, August, https://bijutsutecho.com/magazine/insight/22558

9   Zaman, M., Charbonneau, L. and Maruyama, H. 2003, 'Critiquing the Colonialist Origins of the New National Museum Upopoy', *FOCUS Asia-Pacific*, vol. 107, pp. 9–12, https://www.hurights.or.jp/archives/focus/section3/2022/03/critiquing-the-colonialist-origins-of-the-new-national-museum-upopoy.html

10 Enomoto, I. 2022, '豊穣なアイヌ文化に出会う、道南ミュージアム巡りの旅 〜前編〜', *BRUTUS*, July, https://brutus.jp/ainu_hokkaido_museum1

11 Keira, T. 2018, *The Spirit of Huci: Four Seasons of an Ainu Woman*, Jurousha Co. Ltd., Sapporo, p. 16

12 Clark, J. 2022, 'Cooking in the Ainu Way', *Beshara Magazine*, no. 21, https://besharamagazine.org/well-being-ecology/cooking-in-the-ainu-way/

13 Sasaki, K. 2023, '北海道・阿寒湖アイヌコタンで、北の大地に生きる先人の"知恵"を食す', *BRUTUS*, February, https://brutus.jp/hokkaido_akanainu/?heading=4

14 Sjöberg, K. 1993, *The Return of the Ainu: Cultural Mobilization and the Practice of Ethnicity in Japan*, Routledge, London, p. 54

15 Fujimura, H. 2019, *Shizen no Megumi – Ainu no Gohan,* Dairyman, Sapporo, p.107

16 'Kamuy', *Wikipedia: The Free Encyclopedia*, last edited 23 February 2024, https://en.wikipedia.org/wiki/Kamuy

17 The Foundation for Ainu Culture, 'チュク　チェプ', https://www.ff-ainu.or.jp/tale/details/chukuchepu17.html

18 'エゾシカ', *Wikipedia: The Free Encyclopedia*, last edited 23 January 2024, https://ja.wikipedia.org/wiki/エゾシカ

19 Jalal, I. 2021, 'Hokkaido: A History of Japan's Northern Isle and its People', Earnshaw Books Ltd., Hong Kong, pp. 156–157

20 Ibid., p. 211

21 'アイヌ民族博物館', *Wikipedia: The Free Encyclopedia*, last edited 3 March 2024, https://ja.wikipedia.org/wiki/アイヌ民族博物館

22 Bennett, T. 1995, *The Birth of the Museum: History, Theory, Politics*, Routledge, London, p. 7

23 Kawayu Visitor Center, '弟子屈の歴史・文学散歩', http://www.kawayu-eco-museum.com/english/wp-content/uploads/2019/03/d4ff50ef3e52693b8e059b367fc76585.pdf

24 Matsusaka City Website, 2012, 'Matsuura Takeshiro', https://www.city.matsusaka.mie.jp/site/takesiro/english.html

25 Campbell, K., 2024, 'Manga: Ainu food and remembrance in Golden Kamuy', *Vittles*, March, https://www.vittlesmagazine.com/p/the-story-of-japanese-food-told-through

26 Hatai, A. 2006, 'Materials and Cultures of Foods in Hokkaido Area', *Journal for the Integrated Study of Dietary Habits*, vol. 16, no. 4, pp. 296–301 https://doi.org/10.2740/jisdh.16.296

27 Ipponmatu-umare, 2018, 'ジュンドッグのピジョン館／ジュンドッグ（旭川市・2018.5.ななかまど掲載）', https://ameblo.jp/ipponmatu-umare/entry-12487250464.html

28 Development Bank of Japan, 2019, '北海道のナチュラルチーズ産業の現状と今後の展望〜道内チーズ工房のさらなる発展に向けて〜', March, https://www.dbj.jp/upload/docs/5d2bbeaf76ff89c820857a6f64e86387.pdf

29 '室蘭やきとり', *Wikipedia: The Free Encyclopedia*, last edited 26 April 2023. https://ja.wikipedia.org/wiki/室蘭やきとり

30 JTA Sightseeing Database, 'History of the Maeda Ippoen Foundation', https://www.mlit.go.jp/tagengo-db/en/H30-00043.html

31 University of Michigan Center for Japanese Studies, 'Becoming Marimo: The Curious Case of a Charismatic Alga and Imagined Indigeneity', *YouTube*, uploaded 21 November 2022, https://www.youtube.com/watch?v=YkfrZTli5ew

32 Wakana, I. 2019, 'アイヌの伝説か和人の創作か', *Research Notes of Dr. MARIMO*, January, https://ameblo.jp/maromo-lab/entry-12433135776.html

33 uchukyoku1, '安藤まり子 - 毬藻(マリモ)の歌 (1953)', *YouTube*, uploaded 7 October 2018, https://www.youtube.com/watch?v=KaVvahk4ljo

34 Irimoto, T. 2004, 'Creation of the Marimo Festival: Ainu Identity and Ethnic Symbiosis', *Circumpolar Ethnicity and Identity*, vol. 66, pp. 11–38

35 Happy Pigeon, https://item.rakuten.co.jp/az-pet/fog-0004-2k-normal/

36 Gotōken, 'History of Gotōken', https://gotoken1879.jp/history/

37 Ashibetsu City, '沿革', https://www.city.ashibetsu.hokkaido.jp/docs/5024.html

38 'カナディアンワールド公園', *Wikipedia: The Free Encyclopedia*, last edited 14 March 2024, https://ja.wikipedia.org/wiki/カナディアンワールド公園

39 Hoshi no Furu Sato Ashibetsu, '芦別名物「ガタタン」ってなに?, https://go-to-ashibetsu.com/gatatan

40 'ガタタン', *Wikipedia: The Free Encyclopedia*, last edited 4 January 2024, https://ja.wikipedia.org/wiki/ガタタン

41 Satinover, M. and Satinover, S., 'The Ramen_Lord Book of Ramen', https://docs.google.com/document/d/1qLPoLxek3WLQJDtU6i3300_0nNioqeYXi7vESrtNvjQ/edit

42 Ramen_Lord, 'I went to Sapporo and ate 21 bowls of ramen in 6 and half days. Here's every bowl (and some thoughts in the comments).', *Reddit*, https://www.reddit.com/r/ramen/comments/dqphdr/i_went_to_sapporo_and_ate_21_bowls_of_ramen_in_6/

43 Kushner, B. 2012, *Slurp! a Social and Culinary History of Ramen – Japan's Favorite Noodle Soup*, Global Oriental, Leiden-Boston, p. 91

44 '旭川市', *Wikipedia: The Free Encyclopedia*, last edited 14 March 2024, https://ja.wikipedia.org/wiki/旭川市

45 Moriyama, D. 2022, Hokkaido, Akio Nagasawa Publishing, Tokyo

46 Lewis, A. 2013, 'The Essence of the Japanese Mind: Haruki Murakami and the Nobel Prize', *Los Angeles Review of Books*, October, https://lareviewofbooks.org/article/the-essence-of-the-japanese-mind-on-haruki-murakami-and-the-nobel-prize/

47 Lawrence, K. 'Three nights in Asahikawa', https://murakamipilgrimage.com/three-nights-asahikawa/

48 Leow, F. 2023, 'hello, i wrote a book', *the adventures of furochan*, February https://furochan.substack.com/p/hello-i-wrote-a-book

49 Kushiro Ramen Men'yūkai, '細麺のひみつ', https://www.kushiro-ramen.com/secret

50 Hokkaidō de kurasō!, 2017, '父から子へ、伝承の味「元祖カレーラーメン」【有限会社 味の大王／苫小牧市】', http://webcache.googleusercontent.com/search?q=cache:https://www.kuraso-hokkaido.com/localwork/2017/04/父から子へ、伝承の味「元祖カレーラーメン」

51 '室蘭カレーラーメン', *Wikipedia: The Free Encyclopedia*, last edited 18 November 2023, https://ja.wikipedia.org/wiki/室蘭カレーラーメン

52 Daiou, '味の大王の歴史(室蘭)', http://www.daiou.com/history/daiou_history.htm

53 Daiou, '受け継がれる「大王」流', http://www.daiou.com/img/dousin_2015_2_20_g.jpg

54 See 51.

55 Wakkanai Rishiri Rebun North Hokkaido, 2023, '稚内の"推し麺" ご当地グルメ「チャーメン」を食べに行こう!', https://www.north-hokkaido.com/feature/detail_40.html

56 Tokachinabe, 2019, '初代の味と教えを受け継いでいく。だからぱんちょうの豚丼は旨い!', https://tokachinabe.com/pancho/

57 Hokkaido Labo, 2019, 'シスコライスにステピ?函館市民の青春の味を大調査', https://hokkaido-labo.com/area/hakodate/shiscorice

58 Hokkaido/Sapporo/Dabesa Tsūshin 5, 2016, http://dabesa.sakura.ne.jp/wpkiyo1004-1/1日限定40個の『母恋めし』と『アイヌの物語』

59 Ajanta, 'アジャンタ総本家について', http://www.ajanta.jp/ajanta.html

60 Azuma, H. 2023, *The Philosophy of the Tourist*, Urbanomic, p. 66

61 Ibid., p. 55

62 Demsas, J. 2023 'New York Is Too Expensive to Even Visit', *The Atlantic*, November https://www.theatlantic.com/ideas/archive/2023/11/new-york-tourism-airbnb-rentals-hotels/675860/

63 Saki plus, '【濃厚なめらかプリン】【Creamy Pudding】の作り方/パティシエが教えるお菓子作り!', *YouTube*, uploaded 17 March 2020, https://www.youtube.com/watch?v=LJT_AYIfY_0

64 Yokota, M. 2019, 'パティシエ直伝。おうちで作れる「ドゥーブルフロマージュ」の黄金レシピ', *Macaroni*, https://macaro-ni.jp/73728

65 HidaMari Cooking, 'Double Fromage Cheesecake', *YouTube*, uploaded 17 November 2018, https://www.youtube.com/watch?v=IyKQwjmMDR0

66 Triton Job, '一生勉強、一生青春。二刀流で斬り開く、究極の昆布作り', https://job.fishermanjapan.com/column/1790/

67 Umami Information Center, 'What is Kombu?', https://www.umamiinfo.com/richfood/foodstuff/kelp.html

68 Delish Kitchen, 'あの店の味を再現?!モスバーガーのつくり方', https://delishkitchen.tv/recipes/230500169571894323 (The flavour of that shop recreated?! How to make Mos Burger)

ABOUT THE AUTHOR

Tim Anderson is a chef and author who has pursued an interest in Japanese food for more than two decades. In 2005 he was awarded a research grant to study local foods in Japan, which first prompted his interest in Hokkaido food culture. After relocating to London in 2008, he went on to win *MasterChef* on BBC1, and he has since written seven previous books on Japanese cookery, including *Ramen Forever*, *Your Home Izakaya* and the *JapanEasy* series. He currently lives in South London with his wife Laura, daughter Tig, son Felix and FIV-positive cat Baloo.

いつも

けっぱろう

Published in 2024 by Hardie Grant Books,
an imprint of Hardie Grant Publishing

Hardie Grant Books (London)
5th & 6th Floors
52–54 Southwark Street
London SE1 1UN

Hardie Grant Books (Melbourne)
Building 1, 658 Church Street
Richmond, Victoria 3121

hardiegrantbooks.com

British Library Cataloguing-in-Publication Data.
A catalogue record for this book is available from
the British Library.

Hokkaido
ISBN: 978-1-78488-598-4

10 9 8 7 6 5 4 3 2 1

Publishing Director: Kajal Mistry
Senior Editor: Eila Purvis
Design and Art Direction: Evi O Studio
Copy-editor: Esme Curtis
Proofreader: Sarah Prior
Photographer: Laura Edwards
Food Stylist: Tamara Vos
Prop Stylist: Aya Nishimura
Senior Production Controller: Sabeena Atchia

Colour reproduction by p2d
Printed and bound in China by C&C Offset Printing Co., Ltd.